"Your recovery is remarkabl
you. This comes pretty close to an ᴜnexpectedly great outcome. It was better than
I could have dreamed of!"

—Dr. Judith Shizuru, Professor of Medicine Blood and Marrow
Transplantation, oncologist, and creator of bone marrow transplant received by
author at Stanford Cancer Clinic

"Your complete and sudden recovery from your cancer, which has not
returned at all after it disappeared in 2010, was amazing and unexpected. I am
truly surprised."

—Dr. Baldeep Singh, Professor of Medicine of Primary Care, Stanford
Hospital and Clinics

"While I am not a religious person at all, I do believe that Don's healing was
miraculous and that faith was a critical component."

—Nancy Linford, music educator to children, and cancer survivor

"*Matchbooks in the Tunnel* is both wonderfully written and a gut-wrenching
story of how God instigated a miraculous healing of what had every appearance
of a terminal cancer infection. I offer my enthusiastic recommendation both to
cancer-sufferers or simply anyone who enjoys reading a wonderful story of a
modern-day, miraculous cure."

—Jeff Siemon, four-time National Football League Pro Bowler, 11 year
middle linebacker with the Minnesota Vikings, and inductee into College Football
Hall of Fame; and Director of Search Ministries in Minnesota

"I join Don Mulford in praising God for his remarkable story of healing.
Rather than pit prayer against medicine, or the reverse, Don pursued God's good
gift of healing in any direction from which it might come. In the end, we may
want to ask: was Don healed because of science or because of faith? Yes--that
would seem to be Mulford's dual answer. Sustained by a loving community of
friends, he bears witness to a seamless, intertwining pursuit of the best he could
find in doctors, technology, and insurance providers, while likewise turning to
any noted spiritual practice or reputed healers that might lead him to experience
God's healing power. In the end, Don bears witness to his confident faith God was
the source of his extraordinary outcome, that he receives it as a daily, life-
changing gift, and that he wants to share the story of God's abundant provision.
Amid the myriad sacred and agonizing mysteries and questions of the healed and
the unhealed, I receive Don's witness with deep joy and great thanksgiving."

—Mark Labberton, Ph.D., President of Fuller Theological Seminary and
author of numerous books, including *The Dangerous Act of Worship*

"Don's life and this compelling testimony of a surprising cancer battle victory are poignant reminders that God is still in the miracle business in the 21st century. As a good friend, I had the privilege of seeing this unfold personally. I saw faith, courage, trust, perseverance, committed doctors, and promises from the Bible that anchored him. These are all part of Don's remarkable story. You'll be encouraged by reading it!"

—Mary Schaller, author of *The 9 Arts of Spiritual Conversations* and former president of Q Place

"This is a wonderfully honest and vulnerable description of one person's incredible eleven-year journey of faith as he struggles to embrace physical healing. We are all blessed and encouraged to join Don in this wonderful work of God."

—Doug Burleigh, Associate at Fellowship Foundation (organization responsible for the National Prayer Breakfast) and Former President of Young Life International

"I found Don's book to be a compelling read in many aspects - a stirring autobiographical account of a life-altering health crisis, a whodunit of sorts as Don tries to solve the mystery of his illness, an inspiring story of friends and family coming to his aid, and a deep spiritual conversation about what faith means to him and could mean to all of us. Given I often lean to cynicism and wariness of anecdotes of charismatic teachings and healings, I found Don's account pushing the boundaries of my thoughts by challenging me to consider all possible manifestations of God's plan for us—both as the sick and as the healers. Knowing Don, and his often laid back temperament and sound reasoning, makes this powerful and transformative story especially compelling."

—Kevin Brown, Managing Partner at Jackson Square Partners, LLC, an investment management firm

"Matchbooks in the Tunnel is for anyone who struggles to understand the 'Why' of life's problems, and for those who wish to become more empathetic and compassionate to support others who are in pain. In other words, I believe this book is for everyone. Don's compelling story provides a meaningful role model written in a personally relevant way. Don's influential insights shepherd the reader from an everyday sense of Hope to the depth of Faith in God's personal plan that he has for each of us to truly appreciate our lives and understand our 'Why.'"

—George J. Giokaris, Ed.D., Adjunct Doctoral Professor and Superintendent of Schools (retired)

"Don's journey of perseverance and cancer resonates with anyone who has had to deal with a terminal diagnosis. His roller coaster ride through the many stages of illness, hope, disappointment, and ultimately, healing, is a personal one. Medical science and healing are not separate here but blend into a story that is authentic and engaging."

—Richard Groves, Founding Director of Sacred Art of Living Center, Bend, Oregon

"Mulford, a minister himself, doesn't start with his own deep faith and then merely backfill – in a *deus ex machina* pastoral retelling – in order to explain his path to recovery from terminal cancer, no matter how harrowing the midlife journey indeed was. Instead he steps aside from the pulpit and recounts with inspiration and insight all the compelling details of the hard medical realities he had to face, the enigmatic onset of illness at the start of his ministry, the vital role of family, friends, and community, the devoted doctors who believed in the patient, as well as the Judaean Desert of self-doubt that with any prolonged fatal illness inevitably stretches well beyond 40 days and 40 nights. Finally, authentically, and from the ground up, the reader experiences with the author a profound reconciliation – of the warring elements within the body, of the disparate events that somehow form the arc of one's life, and of status-quo faith itself yielding to what is still possible, life-affirming, and real."

-Lawrence G. Townsend, San Francisco intellectual property attorney and author of *Secrets of the Wholly Grill*

"In this gripping memoir of a decade-long terminal illness miraculously healed, Don Mulford shows honest faith in action. Never sentimental, and with steady hope and a welcome measure of dry humor, he recounts how the illness taught him to partner with the 'wild, loving, surging Spirit of the Living God.' Even more than the healing, that partnership is the paramount gift which sanctifies and extends beyond mortality. Mulford helps us glimpse it through his own wild and precious life."

—Susan S. Phillips, Ph.D., Executive Director of New College Berkeley and author of *The Cultivated Life: From Ceaseless Striving to Receiving Joy*

"This inspiring account of a cancer survivor's medical and spiritual journey during the onset, treatment, and eventual victory over his illness was eye-opening. The author blends his search for answers within his faith with his scientific and medical battle, and makes clear that success in each area was crucial to his eventual cure. It would be an informative read for both the spiritually inclined and those hoping to learn from the example of one man's fight with an affliction so common to our times."

—Rand Herbert. retired consulting historian and graduate seminar instructor of public history at California State University

"Don Mulford is a winsome man of faith who has experienced the worst and the best of encounters with disease and mortality. His testimony is genuine and inspiring."

—Tim Stafford, well known author of numerous books including *Miracles: A Journalist Looks at Modern Day Experiences of God's Power*, Senior Writer for Christianity Today, and winner of two Gold Medallion Awards

"*Matchbooks in the Tunnel* is truly a gentle man's journey through faith to belief, a riveting tale of perseverance and the power of self-persuasion. For one to have so many earnestly well-wishing kith and kin is to be a richly deserving friend indeed, especially in one's own time of need. This late-blooming cleric is such a man, a generous being whose purposeful outward focus on others was involuntarily drawn inward, as if to find the bare root of his pastoral passion. There, by necessity, he digs for redemption from doubt; he does so in hopes of finding new grounds for why he was planted so deeply in the fertile field of his fellow tillers of understanding. There can be no rhyme or reason to why one person and not another kens so clearly the plausibility of parables, so succinctly the suspension of skepticism, or so boldly the beatitude of belief. Illuminated by a literal 'light at the end of tunnel' since childhood, this modest exemplar figuratively penned his path between life's longing for itself and a mission to minister to others. Along the way, his paean of suffering and emergence is as much an inspirational testament for all those who stood by him through his crucible, as it is an indelible exclamatory echo of so many young bulls of men over time who came into maturity many decades before facing the most arduous challenges of their lives. To emerge intact from his cathartic trek through a maze of metaphysical wonderment, unscathed yet oh so deeply touched by unseen forces, is an affirmation of two great forces at work: the author's own capacity to retain an innate determination to be a lifelong learner, and — well-deserved drum roll, please — the strength to bear witness to and so persuasively share what is difficult to comprehend for fellow mortals who have not traveled the same road of recovery to renewal. Norman Doidge has manifestly documented that, 'Nature has given us a brain that survives in a changing world by changing itself.' It certainly appears Don has proven that the same can be said for the human soul. *Matchbooks in the Tunnel* is a cartographic legend by which those brave enough to quest for miracles in their own lives may attain a sentience that serves not only their peers in this world, but also can empower those who encounter the spirit of their stories in times to come."

—Hall Daily, retired government and community relations director at Caltech (California Institute of Technology) and former print journalist

"Don shares his incredible and inspiring journey with readers in an authentic way. His miracle is a reminder to never give up hope - and to rest on our faith in difficult times. I am honored to be a part of Don's life."

—Greg Sampson, eight year offensive lineman National Football League Houston Oilers, voted by the *Corpus Christi Caller-Times* as the Houston Oilers' best offensive lineman in history

"Don Mulford did not set out to be an author, and is humble in his claim to that title. Even so, the calm and level-headed explanation of his unwavering faith and the astonishing history of his victory over cancer is told clearly, and is eminently believable. Do not assume that this is an endorsement of Sunday morning 'televangelical' healing. It is in fact an inspirational and heartwarming narration of the necessity for hope and the power of faith, free of any proselytizing or preaching. Regardless of your own spiritual beliefs you will find much to ponder and celebrate in its pages."

—David Jackson, retired Sales and Marketing Director at Stanford University Press

"*Matchbooks in the Tunnel* is the unvarnished story of a man's search for healing in the midst of being robbed of life by a brutal cancer. Don's tenacious search will touch you but also propel you to find the deep love he found. There are so many profound lessons for everyone in this book, not just those seeking healing."

—Jane Van Antwerp, Pastor of Beyond the Blue Ministries, and Children's Author of *Big Jesus, If We Could See Prayer* and *The Jesus Comfort Quilt*

"Don Mulford's story is one of hope growing into faith, as he faced a diagnosis of cancer. His account describes the frightening adventure of his treatment, and also his growing awareness of God's presence and healing work in his body and life. It's a story he tells with wisdom, generosity and humor. Every one of us knows someone who has fought this battle. Don's book will be a comfort and encouragement to anyone open to a story of faith, courage and miracles."

—John A. D'Elia, Ph.D., President of The New Theological Seminary of the West

"As a retired Idaho Hospital CEO, I fully understand that our healthcare system provides many obstacles to the right care in the right place at the right time. I also appreciate all of the incredible caregivers at Don's bedside who helped him find a cure pathway with a few roundabouts. More importantly, as a cancer survivor myself, I truly believe Don's faith and hope were absolutely critical elements of his treatment plan. In 2008, I was diagnosed with Stage 4 bladder cancer with a 5% survival rate. I'm very blessed to be cured. Faith and hope helped my wife and me on our own journey. I found Don's book very inspiring for all of us who benefit from his inspirations, faith and hope."

—Al Stevenson, CEO, St. Benedicts Medical Center, ret.

"A compelling, authentic book. It is the story of one man's battle with cancer, but addresses with honesty (and sometimes with humor) elemental aspects of the human condition: loneliness, despair, mortality, perseverance, faith, hope, happiness, friendship and love."

—Christopher Avery, international human rights lawyer

"It's been said before, but this truly is a must read. It is a real life, raw journey for anyone going through a health crisis or found themselves questioning their faith. It's also valuable for those supporting someone who is faced with a challenge they never thought they could beat. It shows you how to face unimaginable tests, how we all have our faith tested. It gives the reader knowledge that there is hope and faith despite how dark it may be. Whether you are spiritual or not, this book will encourage you to believe in something greater than yourself. Don, thank you for sharing your journey; doing so will inspire and guide so many others."

—Earl Whetstone DDS

"What a touching story of Don's battle with terminal cancer. From the initial shock of a negative doctor's report, to the daily and yearly struggles, Don presents his very personal journey and persistent desire to win this battle. He masterfully weaves the story to include the elements that added together in his recovery and healing. The support of the medical profession along with family and friends, combined with miracles from God, bring about his amazing victory. It is definitely a story of healing, of God doing the impossible. It is also a story of faithfulness – Don's trusting God, pursuing healing, and prevailing over a death sentence. And finally, it is a story of encouragement that God is love and does miracles for everyone. Great read. Highly recommend it."

—Steven Long, E.D.O.L., Global Champions Ministry, and Victoria Long, MA Intercultural studies

"Don's insights and honesty about his decade-long battle with cancer makes for an inspiring and absorbing read. He has a unique and compelling narrative based on his legal background and enduring faith."

—Jim Dutton, former Supervising Deputy Attorney General, State of California, and author of *Path to Justice*

"Don Mulford's story is powerfully compelling as he shares the intimacies of his agony to ecstasy journey. The inexplicable happened from the dreaded shock of a terminal cancer diagnosis to an out of character search for a miracle. To the surprise of his oncologists and friends, Don is still here to tell his story of hope and healing. This is a must read for all who fear and hear the worst prognosis and enter the unknown twilight zone of uncertainty of life."

—Robert Lincoln Hancock, Author of *Designed for a Purpose* and Founder and President Emeritus of Providence International Foundation Ministry

MATCHBOOKS IN THE TUNNEL

Matchbooks in the Tunnel

How God and Others Solved My Impossible Problem

by Don Mulford

ISBN: 978-1-7349596-0-4

DEDICATION

I have so many people to thank from the bottom of my heart that I will not begin to list them because I will leave someone out by accident. Thank you all who cared for me, prayed for me, loved me, visited me, provided medical care for me, stayed with me, sacrificed for me, and in so many other ways helped me in my hour of need. You saved me. I am forever grateful. Also, thank you God for giving my life.

TABLE OF CONTENTS

FOREWORD

Can Jesus still create miracles today 2,000 years after the crucifixion? The author of this book, Don Mulford, certainly believes this is possible and shares his personal journey of unwavering faith, and what led him to his own remarkable experience. In this must-read adventure you will witness how this miracle occurred and how he brought Christ with him every step of the way.

In Mathew 17:19-20, when Jesus teaches His disciples how to harness this power to heal, it says, "Then the disciples came to Jesus Himself alone and they said to Him, 'Why were we not able to heal him?'"

"Because you have so little faith," He answered. "For truly I tell you, if you have faith the size of a mustard seed, you can say to this mountain, 'Move from here to there,' and it will move. Nothing will be impossible for you."

In the pages of this book, you will see for yourself what these verses truly mean. Being a minister himself, Don already had great faith, but a fight for his life to beat stage four cancer brought him to an entirely new level of faith and a deeper commitment to bring the Holy Spirit into every cell of his body to empower him in every step.

I first met Don back in high school at Piedmont High in Northern California. My dad was a Navy Chaplain at the time and was transferred to Oak Knoll Naval Hospital my junior year. Don and I played on the high school football team together and also hung out in the same group of friends.

The thing that impressed me the most about Don was not only how smart he was, but how much he cared for others. He had a "charge ahead" mentality in everything he did and always found answers when others couldn't, or wouldn't, go the extra mile to find them.

When I heard he became a minister years later, I was somewhat surprised. I'd always thought he would follow his dad into politics. Up until then, I didn't really know the depth of his faith and how it had called him into ministry.

When Don asked me to read his manuscript, I was intrigued, since I too had experienced several very impactful miracles within my own life. In reading about his personal journey through a very challenging situation, I discovered how we had both managed to find a deep and rich relationship with Christ.

Back when I was in college, I was involved in a serious car accident where I was thrown out of a car and into the air only to have it then land on top of me. When the ambulance took me to the hospital I was in really bad shape. My legs had numerous breaks and I was bleeding internally. In other words, I was a mess.

The first hospital decided to transfer me to Oak Knoll Naval Hospital, which was better equipped to deal with my injuries. My dad was the Chaplain there and it was also where they took those who were badly injured from the Vietnam War.

In the ambulance ride between these two hospitals is where I met God face-to-face while I prayed for him to heal me. When we arrived at Oak Knoll, a team of doctors and nurses waiting for my arrival quickly rushed me into the intensive care unit.

When they couldn't find any broken bones or any internal bleeding, they called the doctors at the other hospital to confirm their findings and to make sure I was the correct patient, since they didn't know what to make of the situation.

What they didn't know was that God had healed me in that ambulance ride from one hospital to the other. I never told them, because I didn't think anybody would believe it, and because I couldn't believe it either.

What I know now is, I was afraid others would think I was crazy. So, I just kept it to myself. I went about my life not telling anyone of my experience until nineteen years later at a church retreat where I shared it in a small group setting.

That was my first miracle, now let me share the next one with you. About six weeks before my fourth son was expected to arrive he went into a coma in utero; the doctors gave him no chance of survival. After an emergency C-section, they got him out, but he was lifeless, and they couldn't get him to breathe.

Standing beside my wife, as I wondered if her life was in danger, she said, "I am fine, please go and heal Daniel." So, I moved over to where the doctors were doing everything in their power to revive this shriveled up and deeply blue baby and put my hand on his tiny leg. I said, "Daniel feel my love, and feel God's healing grace." At that very moment, he opened his eyes and began to breathe.

I tell you this now, because when you read this book you might ask yourself is this really possible? Can God still heal as he did with Don, just like the stories we read in the Bible? I myself would have asked these same questions, if I hadn't had my own personal experience of receiving true miracles as well.

So often we let judgment stand in the way of these special gifts.

When you read the pages of this book, you will see how it took an amazing turn of events, an outstanding team of doctors, and Don's "faith as a mustard seed" to create the space for his incredible miracle to occur.

My prayer and hope is that you allow *Matchbooks in the Tunnel* to inspire your life in a way that supports a belief that miracles can happen today, just as they have in centuries past. And to know that in whatever challenge you may face in life, that God is with you, both when you are weak and when you are strong. Know that together you make such a great team!!

Dave Austin, international bestselling author of *The Unfinished Cross: Listen to the Voice Within, Songwriting for Dummies,* and *Be A Beast: Unleash Your Animal Instincts for Performance Driven Results*

PREFACE

I never dreamed that one day a doctor would tell me, "You have cancer." And, "You have eleven or twelve years to live." But like a horrible car accident, the sudden, terrible news smashed into me.

Now I am cured, not merely in remission. How did this great reversal happen? This is the tale.

I found an abiding hope along the way. And I found miracles. Also, I found controversy. I saw some things and went to places which I would never have imagined before my diagnosis.

My goal is not to guarantee anything, describe the right way, or impose any shoulds. I am merely telling what happened and what I found out.

It is all true. I am still surprised.

CHAPTER 1

The Bomb

"You're sick!"

Thus began the conversation with my hematologist upon entering my patient room. He had taken one look at me when he walked through the door and blurted his pronouncement.

For years I had noticed that my weight had evaporated. Blood tests continued to reveal plummeting iron levels. Sometimes I squawked from intense stabbing pains in my waist.

My cardiologist and close friend, Dave, had even exclaimed, "You look like a POW!" After months of plying me with disgusting iron pills, my internal medicine physician gave up and referred me to the hematologist (a blood specialist). It had not taken him long to reach a quick conclusion. Something was wrong.

The hematologist's office sat in one of a group of large, bland buildings which effused, "Prepare to be bored." It brought to mind the sterility of my first dentist's office. These buildings bemoaned, "Abandon all joy all ye who enter here."

The shoebox of a waiting room was packed with patients and families anxiously awaiting their turns. The kind-hearted but stressed receptionist would stretch up from her seat to slide open the opaque plastic window and gasp, "Your name? Please take a seat." Then she would lean back into her chair as the window slid back to its closed position, leaving the patients to step around each other to get to an available seat.

I felt like an animal locked in a cage, waiting for the keeper to toss us some meat. Nobody looked at each other, unwilling and afraid to enter another's misery since we each had enough of our own. Our only relief presented itself in the form of dated, random magazines idling on a rusted rack.

Finally, a nurse guided me to a vacant patient room, which felt vacant. As the waiting room appeared small, the patient room looked huge. I went from a packed room to an empty room, suddenly acutely aware of my aloneness. Whatever malady had found its way inside of me, it was mine alone. The uninhabited patient room seemed to confirm it. This was serious.

Suddenly, an intensely energetic and intelligent looking man in a white lab coat burst into the room, shattering the silence. He threw one glance in my direction and decreed the truth of my suspicions; something was very wrong with me.

Then he did something that nobody had ever done before; he sat down next to me and kindly ordered, "Tell me exactly how you feel." I felt relieved. A new chance to unburden myself from this curse that was causing me to waste away. I gushed forth symptom after symptom, allowing my body to "speak" about its state of being.

I had not comprehended the level of my discomfort, which took over a minute to describe . . . weight loss, pale skin, constant fatigue, and recurrent pain throughout my body. When I stopped, he purposefully got up, strode across the room, and grabbed a very large needle.

He told me to lie down on my stomach on the examination table, which I haltingly did. He rubbed a numbing agent on my lower back, and then stunned me by climbing onto the table and sitting on my back, like a rider on a horse. He forced the needle into my lower back and rocked it back and forth like a rodeo rider on a bucking bronco.

But incredibly, the procedure barely hurt. Yet, it foreshadowed what was to come. Being poked and prodded was to become my way of life. Summarily, he pulled out the needle, stood up, and announced that the appointment was over, "You will hear from me in a couple of days." Then he whooshed out the door.

I thought that I visited the hematologist to get a blood test. Instead, something much grander, yet more mysterious, had happened. I let go of my confusion and uncertainty as I drifted by those in the waiting room, awaiting their turns to find out how sick they were.

I let the experience recede into the archives of my mind as I returned to my daily activity as a relatively new pastor in a nearby church. Two days later, my secretary let me know that a doctor was on the line.

"Hello?"

"You have lymphocytes in your bone marrow, so you have non-Hodgkin lymphoma. You will need to set an appointment to come to see me soon, so we can plan your treatment."

No introduction. No how-do-you-do? "You have cancer," he blundered.

Time stopped . . .

In the movies, you got invited back to a doctor's office for these types of conversations. The anxious doctor would warm you up to the idea, and then compassionately look you in the eyes as you tenderly were told the bad news.

When I had left his office, I did not even know that he was testing me for cancer. He was a hematologist, which meant that he specialized in disorders in the blood ("hema," from "hamia," which is Greek for blood). It did not occur to me that hematologists also specialized in cancer, since many forms of cancer live in the bloodstream.

After he hung up, I literally staggered around my office, acutely aware that my life would never be the same. I was a new and permanent member of the Big C, or cancer, club. I would die much sooner than I expected. All I could do was sit down on my couch. I was 47 years old, and I was going to die. It was 1999.

The youth pastor at our church had told me that the kids thought I was "The Bomb," which in my day meant "cool." I did not know that it foreshadowed a darker meaning of a more malevolent type of bomb, which suddenly had blown up in my head with the shrapnel from the doctor's call.

CHAPTER 2

The Fuse

I stood in front of the church energetically gripping the microphone in my hand. My parents, siblings, and nieces and nephews sat in the seats along with many friends, some who went back to my childhood. And with my "people," the church members sat there with rapt attention, checking out this guy who was their newly installed pastor.

Three of my colleagues had waxed eloquent with flowery comments about me. Now it was my turn. What do you say beyond, "Hi?" But, as I stood there, I felt like finally it was my moment. It had taken decades to arrive at this spot in my career as the Senior Pastor of First Presbyterian Church Richmond in the San Francisco Bay Area. It was 1998.

As a history major at Stanford University, I graduated with a common disease suffered by many of my classmates known as, "I don't know what I want to do now." I teetered back and forth between a hankering to work in some kind of ministry which led people to learn more about God and helping people in a more "practical" way by practicing law.

My father had always wanted me to go to law school which he had attended for one year on the G. I. Bill after serving in World War II. But with a wife and child he had to get a job. He wanted my brother and me to have the chance that he had missed.

He started his campaign to convince me I should be an attorney very early in my life.

When I was in grade school I received my own, personal gumball machine. This clear, plastic sphere full of delightful sugary balls of chewing pleasure sat atop a plastic base which when a penny was inserted and a handle turned caused a gumball to roll down a chute to rest at the bottom. But being entirely plastic, one could jimmy the handle to release a gumball without paying the toll.

I placed this wondrous globe on my small desk where I would dutifully insert a penny from time to time to receive the prized gumball. It was a sweet arrangement until one day I noticed that a substantial number of gumballs had suddenly and inexplicably gone missing. This was disastrous. And there was only one explanation. My older brother had come in the dark of night and removed a handful.

This would not do. I took the most obvious and simplest course of action - I told my father.

I descended the stairs to find my dad sitting alone in his big chair by the fire in the living room reading the newspaper. I approached him slowly and solemnly to set forth the case for the prosecution.

"Uh, Dad . . . "

He peered over his newspaper down at me and intoned, "Yes, Donny?"

"I have a problem."

"Well, what is it?"

"Dave stole my gumballs! There are only half as many as there were yesterday and I didn't take that many. He took them!"

Dave was my oldest sibling. I also had two older sisters, Donna and Patty, but only Dave would commit such a heinous crime.

There it was, well presented in a clear, succinct manner. Justice should be swift now.

My father put down the newspaper on the floor next to the chair and reached down, picked me up, and sat me on his knee. Things were looking good.

Then he looked piercingly and warmly into my eyes and asked, "Where is your evidence?"

Evidence? What was that? I had heard this word several times when we watched *Perry Mason* on our black and white television on Saturday nights. But I did not understand what the word meant.

"Evidence?"

"You want to be an attorney when you grow up, don't you?" Even though I was acting like an attorney in trying to convict my brother I was still thinking of becoming a fireman. I could build some creative fires in the fireplace with pieces of cardboard so working with fire seemed to be an obvious career choice.

"You must have evidence to prove that he took the gumballs." I got the idea - I had to have seen him take them. Well my brother wasn't that stupid!

And suddenly I was being lowered to the floor, aimed toward the stairs, and watching the newspaper being lifted from the floor. Court was adjourned. Case closed. The defense had won without even the defendant having to appear before the judge. Apparently this was the practice of law. Solving problems swiftly albeit not necessarily fairly.

My father's first attempt to attract me to the practice of law had fallen short. But now at this important moment of deciding upon a career path upon graduation from college, I gave law more consideration since it offered opportunities to care for a family and help people. Yet I simultaneously felt a nudge toward a more "spiritual" type of work.

I brought my conundrum to some ministry leaders whom I respected the most. I asked each of them whether I should follow my more vague spiritual inclinations toward theological graduate school or my father's dream of my attending law school. Three leaders said ignore your father's advice and, "Follow God." Three others said the opposite. I had one more person whom I planned to ask.

He was the college pastor at my church. He had invited me into his office and listened attentively to my dilemma. Then he stunned me with the advice, "Do whatever you want to do."

He explained that God was in my decision-making and my desires so I was not disrupting some divine plan whatever path I chose. I felt a huge load lift off of me. And, more surprisingly, I realized that I preferred attending law school. It was something that I understood compared to the more ethereal world of theology.

I ended up joining several of my friends in a law school in San Francisco. After weathering lectures ad nauseam about how property comes from the Latin word res and throwing a rock through a window constitutes a burglary, I ended up working as a government attorney in Los Angeles.

That was the year, 1976, that the original *Rocky* and *Star Wars* movies were released to much hoopla. In my neighborhood, lines of rabid customers ran around the block 24 hours a day to get in to see the movies, after which they would come out of the theater and get back into line to see them again.

I continued to attend church during these years which maintained my interest in ministry. In the hills above my apartment sat Bel Air Presbyterian Church led by the UCLA football star Donn Moomaw. He was an All-American middle linebacker who had played on a national championship team. Having tried to play football in college I liked Donn's powerful presence. He enveloped the pulpit with his large body, long arms, and booming voice. This phenomenon became more personal when I arrived late for a Sunday service.

Donn had already introduced the service when he noticed that all the seats were taken. Unfortunately I was first in the line of folks standing at the door in the back so Donn stopped the service with his thunderous invitation, as he held his meaty hand out to me, "Don . . . would you and the others like to join us here on the steps in front of the pulpit?" What choice did we have? We sheepishly herded down the main aisle and tried to get comfortable sitting on carpeted steps literally at his feet. Then I knew what it must have felt like to be one of Jesus 'disciples sitting at His feet as He taught the masses of people who followed Him.

It was these moments which always made me wonder whether I had chosen the wrong profession. Donn had so much impact on those who attended his church.

As the years rolled by I felt more and more that maybe my suit did not fit. I did not have a passion for the work which my law school friends had. It felt dry. Meanwhile I always seemed to find my way into some type of ministry like volunteering to work with high school kids. I could not help myself.

Also a friend and mentor, Sam Lindamood, would drop by my law office and take me to lunch on the lawn by Lake Merritt in Oakland after I had moved back to the Bay Area. He would simply ask me, "How's your practice going?" He could tell that I was disengaged. He told me he noticed two guys in our town who should be in ministry and I was one of them. He kept at it, taking me to lunch at various places to show me how I could reach people as a minister just as he did as the senior pastor at Piedmont Community Church where I attended growing up.

He was not alone in observing my dejection. A secretary at my law office noticed my anxiety while I was fussing with some documents at the copy machine. She asked me what the matter was. I blurted out that I would rather be a minister which led her to retort, "Then go do it!"

Finally, I did! This decision meant that I had to return to graduate school and start all over again. I chose the well-respected Fuller Theological Seminary in Southern California. Moving back to "SoCal" allowed me to often visit my closest college friend, Doug, who lived in his condo in Malibu across from the beach where James Garner shot *Rockford Files*. Johnny Carson lived nearby on the beach. Brian Wilson of the Beach Boys frequented one of our cafes. If I would study theology I might as well enjoy the good life.

It took many more years to get through seminary, internships, and the hiring process at my new church. But here I stood, excited and fulfilled! I had arrived. It had taken so much time and effort to now stand in front of these people formally installed as a ministry leader.

Following this mountain-top moment I thoroughly enjoyed the experience of serving as a pastor, getting to know the loving people, and preaching from my pulpit. It was engaging, exhilarating, and fun.

But I continued to lose weight and feel poorly which had led to my appointment with the hematologist.

CHAPTER 3

New Normal

"You will live 11, maybe 12, years."

My hematologist/oncologist lectured me about what had become my "new normal," while I sat in a plastic chair in his patient room feeling like I had returned to my elementary school principal's office. He pontificated about how my type of non-Hodgkin lymphoma was identified as marginal zone. It was relatively rare, "It progresses very slowly so we will have some time to treat it. For instance we might try a new experimental drug called Rituximab. Of course there are various chemotherapy treatments we can use."

While he rambled on I slid into an altered state of flatness. My meaningful career, my dependable body, my examination room, my nattering doctor, and my medical plan all became one-dimensional. Even the bland colors of the room blended into a nondescript blah.

"Within a few days, you will have a sample removed from one of your lymph nodes. You will go under general anesthesia. It will take you about six months to get used to the idea that you have cancer. Then it will become normal," he continued.

"It will take another six months after the chemo ends to get used to the fact that your 'new normal 'is living as a person with cancer. Within three to six months from today you will go into remission."

In some kind of internal rebellion to it all I instinctively adopted a psychological strategy to deal with this craziness by asking questions - lots of questions. Later I began taking copious notes of all the answers to my questions which I posed to any medical personnel.

Eventually my pads of questions and notes became a kind of teddy bear, a soft comfort in the pain.

I began my new strategy with my hematologist, "Can I overexert myself? Can I exercise? How much pain will I have? Will I get nauseous? Will I need to wear a wig?" As a retired attorney I intrinsically knew how to come up with more and more questions.

Then I touched a nerve, "May I get a second opinion?"

I suddenly discovered that my doctor highly needed to control the narrative of my cancer. I believed that he had a genuine desire to provide the best medical care that he could for me; he was a doctor! I felt that he truly did not like my driving an hour to Stanford Hospital and Clinics to get a second assessment which in his mind would only make it all more complicated. "Each doctor will have a different opinion and strategy," he said. "It will just get confusing for you and hard for me to treat you. It's better to stick with me."

"What about a bone marrow transplant?"

"No. You can get serious infections and success is unlikely."

After I left his building and drove back to my office my emotional flatness continued. I could not sense any depth to my relationship to God. Rather I felt adrift on a shallow pond.

I continued in my work in a state of functional shock. I had told no one there of my diagnosis because I knew that I psychologically needed to get my arms around the fact that I had a terminal disease. I could not answer the overwhelming empathetic questions such as, "How do you feel about it?" Or, "What can we do for you?" I needed to process and discern my feelings first or I would not escape my emotional numbness while trying to act appreciative and responsive which would ultimately fail.

Therefore I continued in my duties while actually merely going through the motions. I kept preaching on Sunday mornings but my words rang hollow. Yet nobody asked me about it.

My decision led me to not tell anyone else either. I did not want to articulate my feelings about such profound and horrific news until I could truly feel those feelings. The diagnosis stunned me into a deep shock which needed time to recede.

This course of action became a very helpful strategy. It gave me time to assimilate what was going on which prepared me for the forthcoming long and challenging battle. Had I not taken this timeout I believe that my new battle would have become much more difficult.

However this course of action caused an obvious problem; I had no one to help me. This conundrum immediately materialized when I arranged for my biopsy of a lymph node which involved going under general anesthesia. I ended up walking to a subway stop next to my apartment in Oakland to take the train to the hospital. After I awoke from the operation and got dressed I took a taxi back home. This plan worked except for my painful and almost impossible limping up the many stairs back to my apartment.

After two weeks had passed after my diagnosis I recovered from my initial shock. I could at least admit to myself that the news was real. I became more rational again and decided that it was time to arrange an appointment with the supervising minister for our local denomination. He was available to help pastors through difficult issues that would arise.

After quietly settling into a chair in front of his desk I haltingly told him of the diagnosis while he patiently listened. His mature demeanor exuded a comforting air.

I told him that, "My oncologist diagnosed me with non-Hodgkin lymphoma. I have told no one yet because I wanted to get used to the idea before I had to carry anyone else's emotional load. You are the first person whom I have told."

"I am very sorry, Don. That is very difficult news. How are you coping with it?"

I appreciated sharing with someone how I felt inside, "I am still in shock. I know God holds me in His hand, but I don't particularly feel His presence. I am just putting one foot in front of the other."

"That's all you can do. You have received a huge blow. Let yourself have a time to grieve this gigantic loss. You need to take time for yourself."

"I'm not sure what to do next. That's why I came to you."

"Well, that was a good idea. Don, that you need to step down for a while to allow yourself to recover. That's best for everyone, especially you. You can't keep on leading the church while fighting this disease at the moment. You need to give it your full attention. I can find someone to fill in for you temporarily."

"OK. Thank you for your guidance and help."

"You're welcome. I will take care of the church. You take care of yourself."

I did not want to step down. Yet I felt enormously relieved.

I still had to tell the church members. Fortunately the supervising pastor stood with me and even did most of the talking at the following Sunday's service. He already had found someone to replace me which was a surprise to me.

Everyone sat dumbfounded while he shared the news. After the service the church members individually expressed their deep sorrow to me. Then suddenly I was driving home. My new job of fighting cancer had replaced my job at the church.

As I walked in, my apartment felt eerily quiet and empty. No sermons to prepare or meetings to plan. I sat on my couch, alone. I now had a new shock of leaving the church to grapple with. My numbness wrapped around me like a cloak. But even in my shock I sensed God sitting next to me as a silent partner.

With my professional routine now behind me I had no clear path ahead of me. I understood that my new task was to take care of me but there was no plan, no map, no text to guide me in this endeavor. I really needed direction.

CHAPTER 4

My Tunnel

I grew up in a home in a safe corner of the world on a cul-de-sac ringed by tall, sloping eucalyptus trees divided by a lazy creek that ran into a tunnel underneath our home. When walking through the trees I felt like a hobbit in *The Lord of the Rings*, passing through the forest of the ancient trees which talked to each other. The eucalyptus trees next to my home became lanky older brothers and sisters with thin arms that stretched out to protect me from the harsh world above. Their overarching limbs swept downward with a haunting yet restful presence. Because of their close grouping which prevented most of the sunlight from penetrating to the ground beneath they created a gentle haze which warmly invited me into an intuitive conversation with nature while I ambled between them.

The constantly peeling trunks of the trees gave a paradoxical sense of simultaneous death and renewal. They looked old and young at the same time. They offered the wisdom of the ages along with the excitement of newness. They transported me to another time and space when I invaded their world. As I passed around them I felt called to something higher . . . something more.

The shadowy and dank apparitions beneath their limbs offered the unknown, a call to nature's best. Because this misty occlusion prevented full sight, I involuntarily looked within instead of outside of myself. It spoke to the deeper part of me, my better self, of greatness and potential - a call to the future - myself, but more than myself. Each new day of my childhood would press in through their leaves hailing me again with their minty, menthol aroma. Each day offered another journey which began right outside my door.

I lived this mythical journey out on an aptly named street entitled Mystic. It was one block long. It ended at our cul-de-sac where it seemed as if God had said, "I'll give this family a plot of land all their own."

That block on the Oakland/Berkeley border in the San Francisco Bay Area offered smallish, two-story houses from the fifties era. It was snug. The beauty of the neighborhood was the proximity of everyone to each other. I could literally walk out my front door and yell for my friends and enough would race out of their homes to make up two teams for a football game in the street which was just wide enough to accommodate one parked car on each side while allowing one moving car to pass between them.

It was a true neighborhood. People looked out for each other. Parents trusted each other to supervise their kids. We would celebrate the Fourth of July together in our cul-de-sac with a large barbecue and music. When my dad pulled too hard on the front wheel of our large Buick while changing a tire causing the car to fall off of the jack and onto the side of his head the whole neighborhood showed up to take care of him and us until he got better.

A shallow brook known as Claremont Creek trundled and wound smoothly over small stones toward our home until it cascaded into a pool that stepped down to the tunnel where it disappeared. Its opaque, shimmering water seduced me into wanting to follow it into the pensive and private noiselessness of the tiny cave that the tunnel formed. The unexplored dark constantly invited me into its unknown.

My father was a politician. As a state assemblyman he ran for office every two years so his life was always in semi-campaign mode. Part of campaigning meant using marketing tools which included matchbooks with his name and picture on them. This was a time before the concerns of smoking had become accepted. Cigarettes were *in*.

I never quite understood the allure of matches, matchbooks, and by extension, ashtrays, as advertising tools. My father's best friend had worked in public relations. As a present of gratitude to his clients, his friend would give them a large heavy glass ashtray with his name signed on the bottom. Why he would give a dish to someone so they could tip ashes onto his name was something I never could figure out. But what did I know? I was just a kid.

My father's matchbooks had his name and title on the front of them with a friendly reminder to vote for his re-election on the inside of the cover. The idea was for the smoker to feel *good* about him as he or she lit a cigarette or pipe. And for the coup de grâce the smoker would see his picture on the back of the matchbook when he or she put it down.

Because of the hundreds of boxes of matchbooks which he kept in our garage I learned the lessons of subliminal marketing at a very young age. I also learned that I had a limitless supply of fire to light my way through the black cavern beneath the garage. When the call to the darkness overcame me I would grab a couple of boxes of matchbooks to light the way.

My mother kept warning me that some government official upstream might suddenly release hundreds of thousands of gallons of water into the creek that would pour into the tunnel and sweep me out into the San Francisco Bay. That was the best she could do to deter me from some unknown injury during my expeditions.

Sometimes I would take a friend and sometimes I would go alone. To get to the tunnel we had to climb over a wire fence and dance along a concrete lip that stuck out about two inches over the tunnel entrance. Then we would ease ourselves down a concrete wall where we landed on the ground which offered a gentle slope down to the mouth of the tunnel. Once there we would stare into the emptiness and slowly enter. It smelled slightly musty and foul. The small creek dribbled along with a soft clicking sound that broke the silence.

A single match did not offer much illumination against the blackness so we would light a book of matches at a time. Immediately a large flame would flare up producing a broad, gesticulating brightness which lasted for about a minute before it suddenly would burn down and die. The trick was to light the next book from the first book before the darkness enveloped us like a shroud while we fumbled with a new book. When those inevitable moments happened we would hear the ripple of the creek against the concrete and feel the gentle, cool breeze running through the tunnel - eerily and forbiddingly. Finally when we used the last book in a box we would crush the box and set it aflame like a torch.

We never became expert at planning our trips nor did we even know how long the tunnel ran. Invariably we had to turn back before reaching the elusive end of the tunnel. Usually we waited too long so we did not have enough matchbooks to keep the path lit on the way back. The tunnel changing directions compounded our problems so we could not merely turn around and see the light at the entrance to the tunnel. When the matches ran out it forced us to edge our way back along the tunnel's wall. Somehow we always made it back safe and sound.

Looking back I found that the continual return to the tunnel shielded by those beautiful eucalyptus trees was part of my youthful search for more of life, the adventure into the unknown . . .

With my abyss of a cancer diagnosis I subconsciously harkened back to those years of exploration into the tunnel as I sought answers in my life-and-death darkness now. How could I find life and *more* in this new black tunnel of cancer?

Over time it slowly dawned on me that Someone had been with me in the tunnel long ago even when I was alone. This sudden dark void of solitude of spirit caused by my diagnosis reminded me to recognize that Person at my side then and now.

I discovered that I did not so much have a direction now but a companion which made this darkness more habitable like the sense of comfort that I always felt, despite the darkness, in the tunnel and when walking under the eucalyptus trees which guarded it.

CHAPTER 5

Talking to Myself

Cancer is a very personal experience. I did not get cancer along with a group. I did not catch it from someone else. It started in me and stayed within me. It was all mine. I was alone with it.

Nobody could get into where I lived - not a parent, not a spouse, not a friend. The physicians had treatments for my cancer but they could not put their hands inside of me and make everything better. Only God could meet me within. I found solitude in my illness and found God in my solitude.

Shortly after I left the church I sat in my car parked in a shopping mall where I had just left a store. I could not reach for the ignition with my key. The bleakness had caught up with me.

I was in the prime of life, my forties. I had recently landed in my career path after decades of effort to get there. This was not the way it was supposed to go. I finally had found my place in the world. And now I would die.

The news had mauled me. I sat in my misery.

To my right the sun slid toward the horizon coloring the parking lot with a tan haze that accented the shallowness of the setting. Lonely, empty cars sat facing me while surrounded by faded storefronts. Like the view from my windshield I too was fading.

The car's interior confined me into the tight contour of the seat on my larger back. My own body confined me with the terminal cancer running through me. I gloomily sat in my trap.

"Really?"

I peered up at God while sitting and waiting. Noiselessly.

I was not normally a *why?* kind of person. I accepted things as they came. I assume that I integrated this philosophy from my mother who usually went along with the flow. She used to say things like, "It was meant to be," with a wistful wave of her hand.

My mother countered my father's bombastic energy with a soothing calm. She provided peace amid our life storms.

But slumped in my car seat that afternoon I could not ignore the agony from the loss of my health and the life that I had expected to live. The ugliness was coming into focus. I wanted some kind of explanation. My plans and hopes . . . how was my faithful God taking care of me now? I did not deserve this unwelcome and fatal disease.

I ached deep down in the tunnel of my soul. Rather than overwrought I felt dismayed. I had lived my life expecting things would sort of work out, that I was part of a cosmic plan. But the script suddenly had been rewritten and I no longer knew my lines. I sat there staring out the window, puzzled.

I did not receive an answer but slowly I noticed a subtle nudging of God's loving presence within me. It surged incrementally with an anticipation and energy that led to my understanding that we could and would get through this thing together somehow.

Any sense of possibility of betrayal by God began to evaporate at that moment. I inherently knew that once again God was the One in this tunnel with me. The cancer had not caught Him by surprise. Somehow it would be okay.

I did not plan to sit there in the car for an hour. But I was glad that I did. My grief was bubbling up from the well deep within me and needed to pour out. It did not come in tears but in a frank admission to myself of the reality of my desperate situation.

As that flowed up and out I could then feel that presence beneath the pain. I realized that I had experienced this spiritual presence, in one form or another, all my life. Now it again appeared in unseen yet palpable fullness. As I made space for God in my spirit by giving into my feelings I found God moving into the vacated space.

Finally I could reach my ignition key and so I started the car. As I drove home with the sun settling into the Bay in front of me I observed a resigned tranquility inside of me. I had faced down The Question with God . . . Why?? I heard my answer. Somehow it was going to work out. I was not alone. We would get out of this tunnel together.

Shortly after this time in the car my evenings changed. The worst part of the day (the darkness and aloneness of night) reversed into the best time. When I got into bed I could palpably feel Jesus' arms around me hugging me. I felt cozy and warm - every night. From then on I slept contented.

Sometimes I journaled about these recurring moments of oneness with God. Converting thoughts into words as I filled pages in my journal added focus and clarity to my experience:

Solitude is to experience the joy of Him, not a vacant emptiness.

The purpose of solitude is to grapple with and trust God for real.

Silence or solitude - silence is different from solitude. Silence causes fear but solitude includes God's presence which provides help for the problems.

Pope John Paul II lost his mother, father, and only sibling in his youth. He was alone but not lonely. He wrote that he found God in his loneliness. He was energized by his praying. So thank God for cancer because it paradoxically leads to good, that is to God. God is saying, 'You don't know your future or what wonderful plans await. Be more Mine. I am your center, your identity. I will provide.'

Now that I found that I was not alone in my darkness I saw cracks of light in my tunnel.

CHAPTER 6

Power!

When I was in seminary in the late 80s my uncle invited me to attend a healing service at his church in nearby Glendale. After the guest speaker explained how God heals people today he invited people to come forward for church members to pray for their healing. I had listened with dubious attention and now wondered if I should go forward.

First I did not really have anything wrong with me besides a trick knee. But then again I was in seminary where I was learning about all kinds of new spiritual concepts so experimenting with physical healing would serve as good field training.

I slowly stepped up the stairs onto the stage where a woman about my age asked if I would like prayer. I directed her attention to my knee.

I uncomfortably stood in front of her while she reached down and held her hand two inches from my knee while she prayed. After a minute of silence she straightened up and proclaimed that, "I can't get through. You need to have a guy pray for you."

I did not know that healing prayer was gender based. Nor did I know that it was about "getting through" to something or somewhere. I stuck around and let a guy pray for me but my knee did not feel any better. So much for healing prayer.

But several years later I gave it all another try. I attended a gathering which offered John Arnott, founder of the Toronto Airport Vineyard Church where many incredible healings happened. After his introduction John sauntered onto the stage looking like a giant, rumpled bear in his overalls. He spoke simply and kindly describing the depth of God's love for us and the magnificence of His power.

After his talk he suddenly enthused, "Okay, let's pray for healing for something. How about heels?"

His sudden and off-handed introduction of healing took me aback. He planned to pray for heels of all things. Surprisingly two people came forward with complaints about heel injuries.

One woman grimaced as she slowly clumped to the front in heavy orthopedic boots. She told John that she needed to wear them because of her fall from a ledge which had smashed both of her heels.

He did not make a big deal out of his prayer for her. He comfortably placed his hand on her head and said, "Heels be healed in Jesus ' Name." That was all.

Then she perked up. She started walking more energetically and eventually began jumping up and down with a gargantuan grin on her face.

Wanting to confirm the authenticity of her healing I looked over at the group with whom she had been sitting rather than at her. Her friends looked in awe and surprise at her antics. Apparently her healing was genuine.

I had never seen a miracle like this especially one that had happened so quickly and spontaneously. Apparently physical healing happened sometimes.

But now the idea of God healing people became much more personal.

After my self-conversation in my car I noticed the name of Benny Hinn blazing across the huge sign standing next to the Oakland Arena within a few miles of where I lived in Richmond.

I had heard of Benny Hinn, a controversial worldwide preacher whose splashy, showboat style had led some to disbelieve the alleged healings at his meetings. (Years later, I spoke with a pastor colleague whom I trusted. He had travelled for seven years with Benny Hinn, handling logistics at the large meetings. He told me how he carefully had watched all the people offer their claims of healing and found that their healings had happened.)

Considering my overpowering diagnosis I considered attending one of his meetings at the Oakland Arena. Subconsciously I tinkered with the thought that perhaps my diagnosis and future were not so bleak. I even allowed the possibility of my healing to enter into my mind.

I believed in God. In fact I had a very personal relationship with Him. He had seen me through some rough moments in the past. And now this purported healer was on the way . . .

While waiting for an appointment with my hematologist/oncologist, I struck up a conversation with a patient named Pam. An English woman about my age, she had suffered from a very serious form of stomach cancer for several years.

Because I was a minister we talked about issues of faith. Pam said that she had grown up Catholic but did not practice her Catholicism. I told her about the arena sign with Benny Hinn's name and how I had decided to go to a meeting. Surprisingly she wanted to join me.

Going to the Oakland Arena for a healing service carried heavy psychological freight for me. The arena sat next to the Oakland Coliseum which housed many wonderful memories of my father and me attending Oakland Raiders football games. I had never forgotten them. My father and I often struggled to converse but we loved going to those games together. He even knew the owner and some players who had been fun to meet.

Pam and I showed up with curious and hopeful hearts. Thousands of people packed the floor and most of the balcony in the humid, energized arena. Pam and I found some seats in the balcony. The hurts and hopes of the participants radiated from the floor as the singing began. I had never heard hymns sung so tenderly or imploringly. I could almost taste the palpable, unified ache of these thousands of people.

As the music subsided Benny sprang through a 12-foot arch on the back of the stage in his all-white suit. He immediately intoned his allegiance to Jesus Christ to Whom he gave all the glory. He then calmly shared a story from the Bible about God's power and compassion in performing miracles.

When he finished, with no invitation or explanation, people started streaming forward to tell about their healing at the meeting. They stood in a long line by the side of the stage awaiting their turn to tell about their miracle. Pam and I looked at each other; then we looked at the people on stage; then we looked at each other again; and shrugged our shoulders. We watched closely. Everything appeared spontaneous, natural, and authentic.

The room throbbed with all the commotion of hundreds of people milling around. Benny or a member of his staff individually interviewed each person who came forward.

"I don't know. I could not stand up straight for ten years but while you were speaking my back just straightened all on its own."

"I fell a few months ago and hurt my knee real bad. I could barely walk on it so have been using this cane. But tonight the pain has gone away completely. I don't need this cane anymore." She left the cane on the stage and walked down the stairs to her seat.

Another person claimed that his stomach cancer was healed during the meeting. He said that he no longer felt any of the symptoms which he had so intensely felt for so long.

Dozens of people offered similar stories. I did not discern any hype or phoniness despite the drama of it all.

Then it was over. Benny disappeared through the arch and the stage emptied. Everyone slowly exited the arena.

Pam and I eventually made our way downstairs. We walked onto the main floor of the arena which was now virtually vacant.

Unexpectedly Pam confided to me in a hushed voice, "There is power in this room."

Her comment dazed me. She had not previously conveyed any inclination toward the spiritual so for her to make such a statement caught me off guard. Then immediately I sensed deep within me that if she could feel it maybe it all was real. Maybe healing worked like it apparently did for the people who had just described their healings.

Perhaps . . . God could heal me. I started to get excited for the first time since my diagnosis.

I dropped Pam off at her home and drove home in a bewildered, lighter mood. I decided to return the next night to watch it again. I got there earlier and found a seat in the balcony closer to the stage. To sit on a chair on the main floor would have necessitated arriving in the morning and I did not feel well enough to do that.

I sat down next to a man who apparently had suffered a stroke; his left arm drooped by his side. He told me that he was very hopeful about being healed that evening. The program began with music and followed essentially the same format as the prior evening. At the close of the talk people again started coming forward. More people told of amazing healings that had just occurred. Then something even more incredible happened.

Caught up in the enthusiasm of the moment Benny bounded to the middle of the stage and threw out his hands toward the people sitting in the front yelling, "Power!" He looked like the emperor in the last of the first trilogy of *Star Wars*, *Return of the Jedi*, where the emperor shoots lightning bolts toward Luke Skywalker, who is plaintively calling out, "Father," to Darth Vader.

Suddenly about 30 rows of people looked as if they were pushed back very forcefully into their seats by a gale force wind that almost lifted them out of their chairs. They could not control this invisible pressure against them. This bizarre phenomenon lasted maybe 10 seconds.

Then he quickly pivoted and in the same way thrust his hands toward the two-hundred person choir sitting in the balcony behind the stage. "Power!" Again they all were pressed into their seats the same way.

With the number of people affected by this power and the spontaneity of the moment it could not have been choreographed. Some force had overpoweringly pushed them into their seats.

I could not believe what I saw but there was no mistake. It had happened. I sat there dumbfounded. Who was this guy? I had seen nothing like this before.

I thought that if someone had this kind of power from God then the healings over the last two evenings must have been real. And yet the man sitting next to me was not healed, to his obvious disappointment. Then it ended suddenly like the night before.

I drove home with my hopes and my questions. But I could not dismiss what I had seen - twice. Pam had been right. There was some kind of enormous spiritual power at those meetings which manifested in the form of healing of very serious maladies.

My sudden, terrible diagnosis had slammed me. But within months I had experienced and seen unbelievable, miraculous healings in my hometown in a very familiar venue. My prognosis was terrible but something even more wonderful had arrived on my doorstep.

This was a common way in which God had worked in my life in the past, using something incredible and personal to me to let me know that He was on the job, fixing my impossibly bad situation.

In my journal that evening, I wrote:

Healing is a relationship with God . . . smiling and not angry, not unapproachable. I am so loved, so invited. All is okay . . . I'm not cancer free yet, but will be.   Seeing God work will be out of my comfort zone and inconvenient, but not impossible. I will have to press through by prayer and action. Cry out for miracles . . . Get uncomfortable.

"Uncomfortable" was the perfect word. I could not explain what I had witnessed. It seemed to only occur for some, which I did not understand. Yet still it had apparently happened.

I arrived at the realization that I just may have a way out of this mess. I did not have answers to my questions but I had hope for a potential miracle. God could heal me. This possibility had appeared on the radar screen of my consciousness. I was approaching a threshold of the supernatural into a new depth of trust in my relationship with my loving God.

I decided to pursue it.

CHAPTER 7

Mentors and Roll Models

One evening, I received a call from an older gentleman in Southern California who identified himself as Gene. He politely said that my beloved cousin Millie had asked him to call me. She and I were very close; I knew that after she had heard about my news, she deeply grieved over my diagnosis.

According to Gene, Millie had approached him at their church and told him about my plight. She knew that Gene regularly visited retirement homes to pray for residents. He also served in a ministry for men. He promised her he would call me to ask if I would like him to pray for me.

In the quietude of my apartment any call was welcome.

"Hello, is this Don?"

"Yes . . . "

"Hi Don, my name is Gene. Your lovely cousin Millie asked me if I would call you. I attend the same church as she does. She knows that I reach out to folks to offer prayer, so if you would like, I would be happy to offer prayer for you from time to time . . . if you like."

"Sure! Millie is such a sweet lady. She is more like my aunt because of our age difference. I would really appreciate any prayer you want to offer."

"Well, tell me how you're doing. How can I pray for you this evening?"

And so began a decade-long ongoing conversation with my newly found brother who not only would call regularly to check up on me and pray for me but even invited me to leave voicemails on his phone every night with messages about my condition. Then he would pray for me on the following morning during his regular prayer times.

This constant communication with a man who became my mentor and confidant was an emotional lifeline that walked me through some hard times.

Gene had grown up as an orphan which had led to a rather untamed lifestyle for decades. Recognizing his emptiness and confusion he asked Jesus to help him out. This act of faith gave him the security and acceptance of unconditional love which he had craved. He knew what loneliness and fear does to a person which gave him tremendous empathy for those in retirement homes and with serious illnesses.

We grew very close in our dozens of conversations. Finally we met at a conference at Lake Tahoe. We warmly embraced and then sat down to take our friendship to a new altitude. Someone took our picture with a bent, balding elderly gent next to a very thin, pale middle-aged man. We both beamed into the camera arm in arm.

Back at sea level my brother counseled me, "If I were you, I would buy a big poster of Lance Armstrong and put it on my bedroom wall."

My brother was an exerciser. He once had run five marathons in five months and regularly outraced cyclists half his age in 100 mile rides. Lance was one of his role models especially since he had defeated his own terminal cancer.

He called me during the glory years for Lance Armstrong, before his admission of using performance enhancing steroids. Lance was at the top of his cycling career at the time that an oncologist diagnosed him with metastatic testicular cancer which was usually fatal. He had found success on the cycling circuit and was on his way to winning the Tour de France, the most difficult cycling race in the world. To defeat his cancer he suffered through an intense form of treatment. He was the perfect poster boy for my wall.

I did not buy the poster but I got the book - his autobiography about his cancer journey, *It's Not About the Bike: My Journey Back to Life*. I read it from cover to cover. I looked closely at the pictures of a very strong, and then very sick, dude.

It struck him at the age of 25 with stage three/advanced testicular cancer which had moved to his brain, lungs, and abdomen. His urologist later said of his chances, "Almost none. We told Lance initially 20 to 50% chance mainly to give him hope. But with the cancer he had, with the x-rays and the blood tests, almost no hope."

He chose the most aggressive form of chemotherapy and surgery. Incredibly within five months after his diagnosis, his oncologist declared him cancer free! He was back on his bike in serious training within a year.

He won! He won . . . He won . . .

Cancer had knocked him flat but he had muscled his way to victory - literally. Not a bad role model for someone who was told that cancer would kill him. I was looking for a role model who, like a friend who told me after his Parkinson's disease diagnosis, "I will kick its butt!" Or as our football coach would exhort us, "Hit it in the mouth!"

My mother was the calming spirit on one side of the parental coin of my life while my father was the battling spirit on the other. Gene presented my mother's firm steadiness. Lance conveyed my father's never-say-die aggressiveness.

A year after his diagnosis Lance set up the Livestrong Foundation to provide psychological support for cancer patients. Stanford Hospital and Clinics took part in his program which led to Lance visiting the hospital. His autographed picture adorned the wall in the cancer clinic where I eventually would visit. I felt a surge of inspiration every time I walked by it.

Lance's organization even sent out yellow rubber bracelets which exhorted, "Livestrong." I got mine and wore it all the time. Every time I felt it or saw it I remembered that Lance had beaten his terrible cancer. So could I.

Lance had appeared on *The Late Show With David Letterman*, where David asked him if during the cancer he had ever thought of quitting.

"Oh no," he quietly responded.

"That's great! That's great!" exclaimed David.

I loved it because I needed it - a celebrity on national television who had talked about how he had prevailed over his terrible cancer. Nine months into my cancer at the beginning 2001 I wrote in my journal, *I saw Lance on TV last night. He's a cancer SURVIVOR! I could see it in his eyes.*

Five months later I wrote in my journal, "Lance is a survivor," after reading the fifth chapter of his book, "Conversations with Cancer."

Lance's disillusioning confession that he had used performance-enhancing steroids thankfully came after my recovery yet it did not change the fact that he had beaten cancer with cancer drugs, not performance enhancing steroids. In addition he had used his celebrity to help thousands of cancer patients like me to find hope from his example, while raising money for cancer research.

His generous heart led me to share in his competitive spirit that had overpowered cancer with grit and guts. He psychologically breathed into me hope that I could do the same when I needed all the hope I could muster.

As I pursued healing I slowly learned that hope was the key. Anything that raised my hope level pointed me toward a state of trust that healing would happen, that God somehow could miraculously intervene.

I found that hope came in many forms. Sometimes I found it in the mystic coolness of God's presence as I had felt when walking beneath the shade of the eucalyptus trees and in the dank tunnel of my childhood. Sometimes I found it in witnessing the miraculous healings of others. Sometimes it was in encouragement of friends, especially in their assurance that they were praying for me. And sometimes it was in dramatic stories of those who rolled over cancer with brutal courage, like Lance Armstrong. All of these moments gave me hope.

CHAPTER 8

A Lighthouse

"Stay away from people."

This was my oncologist's mantra for months because of my depressed immune system. He wanted to prevent my coming down with a serious bronchial infection. Finally he relented and said 15 minute visits with friends was okay. Eventually this led to his allowing me to join a support group.

After some online research I found a cancer support group network which offered to provide an environment for cancer patients to meet for mutual encouragement.

I found the nearest office about an hour from my home; I eventually dropped by. The spacious office contained many tables and open areas lined with shelves full of books and tapes about cancer. It looked like a great resource for research if I only had the energy to get myself there to use it.

The receptionist kindly informed me that one could not walk into a support group meeting like with Alcoholics Anonymous. Rather I had to go through a screening process of two interviews before they would allow me to attend a group meeting.

For my first interview I returned to the office. They shepherded me into a small, hazy, and airless room crammed with a table and some chairs.

As time went on I developed an enduring dislike for confining, drab rooms which drained my spirit.

My anxious host quietly slipped into the room. She benignly introduced herself and informed me she had suffered through breast cancer from which she had gone into remission a decade earlier. She asked me about my cancer before reiterating her constant fear of her breast cancer returning. She mused, "Our time on earth is limited like sand in an hourglass."

I assumed that a support group was for sharing each other's burdens but I thought it was strange that my introductory interview would end up with my providing emotional support to my interviewer about her fear of a cancer that she did not even have at the moment. At the end of our time together she approved my continuing the interview process.

The second interview necessitated my third hour-long drive in each direction to the office at which I had not even attended a group meeting yet. Two people interviewed me this time, one of whom barely introduced herself while the other one gushed with joy and optimism which she claimed arose from her gratitude to God for her remission. She was the polar opposite from my first interviewer. I wished that I had started with her.

They asked questions about my diagnosis, my expectations from attending the group meetings, and my emotional state. I honestly told about my fears and my hope that the group meeting would lift my drooping spirits. They both approved my attending the group meetings.

Unfortunately the group meetings took place in the same office during the evenings when I was the most fatigued. Yet I made my way to my first meeting. Upon entering the room I located a seat around the perimeter of the large circle of chairs and sofas.

The large room held approximately 40 people who presented a broad spectrum of the human condition. Some appeared to be interested, some depressed, some exhausted, and some hopeless. The general mood was somber interspersed with moments of lightness.

In the middle of the circle our leader, a licensed psychologist, languished on a couch. She appeared more prone than upright in body and in spirit, an apparent mix of fatigue, burnout, and apathy. Maybe she subconsciously was mirroring back to us what she sensed but it lowered the spirit of the meeting even more.

People spoke spontaneously after introducing themselves. The psychologist played referee, making sure that people spoke politely and did not proselytize or attempt to convince anyone that they had the answer to cancer.

We were there to find emotional support but disappointingly I did not feel supported. Perceptible anxiety permeated the room heightened by the crowded feeling of so many people packed together. We seemed too overwhelmed by our own distress to convey much hope to each other.

However one man who spoke more often than anyone else struck a different note. He more shouted than spoke regaling us with the good news that despite his doctor predicting that he would pass away on this very day, "Here I am!"

He seemed to take a shine to me, addressing several of his comments to me, always beginning them with, "Pastor!" We sat directly across the room from each other so everyone witnessed his monologue confessional.

"Pastor, nobody knows what it's like until the doctor tells YOU that YOU have cancer!" I nodded in affirmation.

My heart went out to these good people. I could identify with them. Then a young woman to my left introduced herself as a new attendee like myself.

"I have just been diagnosed with breast cancer."

Like me she manifested a paradoxical enthusiasm which I think came from the adrenaline rush that first accompanies a cancer diagnosis. Along with the shock my diagnosis had brought a major surge of energy from my body's impulse to fight back. Despite my bad news I had experienced a high from that energy surge.

Then she continued, "But my faith is sustaining me."

At this moment the psychologist rose from her repose on her perch and sniffed, "Well that works for YOU . . ." Then she returned to her prone position.

I understood that we were not to sell our personal beliefs. But this woman had just been diagnosed and was honestly sharing with this new group how she was dealing with it. She was not proselytizing.

As I drove home I felt hurt and angry. I realized that I needed a place where I could verbally process my confusion in safety. I was there for support - as is. That was the purpose of a group - to support me. I felt that this group, or at least its leader, would judge me whether or not intentionally. I would have to be very careful about what I said when processing my feelings. What was the point in that?

The cancer diagnosis had created a substantial upheaval in my spirit. I knew that I was very sick. I now believed that God did miracles. I hoped with increasing fervency that God would do a healing miracle for me. However the search and waiting for a miracle came with emotional highs and lows. I needed that which would provide me hope and stability which was what a support group was all about.

I looked for something else. Then as seemed to happen often during these days I somehow heard about a group at a nearby church where I had formerly attended, First Presbyterian Berkeley. The group boasted the intriguing name Lighthouse to shed light in the darkness of serious illness. Located only a few miles from my childhood home the group renewed my experience of the tunnel under my home.

An upbeat pastor named Debbie, who was always pleasant, centered, and able to engage everyone with a smile, made me feel welcome and accepted as she led the group. In her presence I felt the comfort and safety which I sought.

We met in the church's oldest building in a musty room of century old paneling holding old books on old shelves. We sat on broken down couches resting on faded carpet. Again I felt my childhood home's eucalyptus trees offering a mystical call to the wisdom of the ages. The safety and spirituality under those tree limbs lived in this dusty old room.

The oldness spun off a feeling of the presence of the prayers and love of thousands of members who had used that room through the past decades. God was there.

The group projected, even radiated, hope. The stark contrast between the mood of the two groups was startling. This small group of six very sick people projected unforeseen energy and enthusiasm. In fact it reflected expectancy. It embodied genuine trust in God's love and a certainty that the best was yet to come.

When I first arrived a very seriously ill middle-aged man, planted in his wheelchair, told me with an ebullient smile that his time was short, "I feel like a child sitting in the hallway waiting to go into the ball!" His sense of hope overwhelmed me.

The entire group emanated this same sense of hope sort of shimmering in the musty room. There was a weightiness in the air. Everyone greeted me with a genuine smile when I first arrived. I immediately felt welcomed and included.

We met every two weeks to talk over how we lived and struggled. We shared about our treatments, our pains, our hopes, our dreams, and our families. We talked, laughed, and prayed. For some reason we never seemed to cry. It was a wonderful respite despite all our underlying woes.

The weeks raced by. I could weather the first season of my cancer with its challenging treatments largely because of the Lighthouse group. Some people came and some people went. Some eventually died which led us to celebrate their entry into the *ball* in heaven.

I found sanity and safety there that stood against the instability and chaos of the rest of my life. I was known and understood despite being a pastor with cancer. I fit.

I wrote in my journal after a couple of these friends had passed:

Once I will pass from this life; now I am peaceful, light, happy, loving, and strong.

This friend was like a song - powerful, light. She was a servant who put others first which is why she was so strong in the Spirit. She is that rock on my walk - with a stream over it so I can't see the rock but it is there.

These friends became my heroes.

CHAPTER 9

Initiation

The word chemotherapy comes from the same root word as chemistry, the study of how substances interact, combine, and change. Since cancer comprises the harmful, abnormally fast growth of cells which can unnaturally invade parts of the body, chemotherapy interacts with the cancer cells with poison to slow or stop their growth.

It is a lousy idea because it kills cells somewhat indiscriminately which means it also kills good cells. However it lengthens patients ' lives because the cancerous growth of cells slows down. My oncologist planned to use chemotherapy (chemo) to slow the expansion of my non-Hodgkin lymphoma for as long as possible.

I originally considered skipping chemo since it would harm my body. Also the question of faith arose. Could not God just heal me without all these nasty drugs? I answered myself that He could. This presented a very important dilemma that I had to resolve quickly.

I experienced my relationship with God as an abiding, ongoing connection, which manifested itself in my real life. I found that God usually used ordinary means to take care of me. Instead of healing my broken arm instantly, He used a doctor who set the broken bone and put it into a cast for six weeks. Yet God occasionally intervened instantaneously when He supernaturally caused healing, as with the woman with the crushed heels.

Also I believed that my life with God was a co-partnership where my decisions and His affected the outcome of my problems. Therefore in my current life-and-death scenario I had a choice whether to use common medical practices or to wait entirely on God hopefully to heal me in a more dramatic fashion.

After prayer and what World War II hero Jimmy Doolittle had called, "Giving it a good think," I concluded that since God's Spirit lived in me I trusted that His Spirit influenced my judgment and decision-making. I could trust that God's presence in me would intuitively influence my judgment. Like when I decided to go to law school, I went along with whatI *wanted* to do. Here I felt better about taking the chemo so I did, trusting that God was in that decision.

With the beginning of chemo, I crossed over a kind of psychic line within myself. I gave up any denial of the fact that I really had a terminal disease and now fully embraced its existence in my body with all its torturous manifestations.

Life is full of initiations like starting a new school. Yet there was something spooky about initiating myself physically into a deliberate poisoning of my body by my hand. Added to this ghoulishness I had to watch it unfold slowly and drastically right before my eyes. But then again since I still was in some state of functional shock from the diagnosis allowing chemo into my body did not bother me as much as I thought it would.

I returned to my oncologist's office on the *Big Day* where the nurse ushered me into a much smaller room than my original patient room. Heaving with cabinets on rollers and other medical supplies the room housed a variety of unfamiliar aromas wafting around me.

I shoehorned my body into a plastic chair that sat against one wall. I brought along my Southern California friend Doug who had arrived in town the day before to meet with a business colleague. He squeezed into another chair as the nurse carefully affixed into my arm a needle attached to tubing that ran up a pole to the bag of chemotherapeutic liquid.

We all intently watched in pregnant silence as the liquid dripped and oozed menacingly toward my arm. Then . . . it crossed the threshold and I would never be the same. The procedure inaugurated me into the world of chemo.

Strangely I did not feel much of anything during or after the infusion. It all happened steadily, quietly, and almost reverently.

Eventually the bag emptied. We murmured to each other as the nurse removed the needle. Then Doug and I removed ourselves from the premises. We did not say much. The moment demanded reflection rather than comment. I knew that something quite profound had happened to me despite transpiring smoothly.

Doug briefly wished me well and left to meet his colleague. I drove home feeling indescribably different. I already had the toxic agent of cancer in my body; now I had two.

The chemo never brought much pain through the weeks that followed. However it often felt uncomfortable and sometimes even intolerable. By definition it was a foreign agent in my body so my body accordingly did not want it there.

After some time my oncologist did not like my testing results so he pushed beyond the normal six rounds of chemo in order to, "Knock it out." I did not know then that his strategy would harm me more than help me.

CHAPTER 10

Sanctuary

I had chosen my oncologist because his office sat near the office of my internal medicine doctor who had referred me to him. I was at the complete mercy of the advice of this oncologist who not only cared for lymphoma patients but many patients with different types of cancer. I decided to call two close doctor friends from high school and college for additional advice.

Dave was the lead cardiologist at the main hospital in Oakland. Paul was a radiologist at the Oakland Children's Hospital. Both had graduated at the top of their classes so fully understood the medical game of which I knew nothing.

In my first conversation with Paul he immediately suggested that I switch to an oncologist who specialized only in lymphoma cases. My present oncologist could not keep up with as much of the latest research nor garner as much necessary experience as someone who specialized in only my type of cancer, non-Hodgkin lymphoma.

Paul even volunteered to make several calls to colleagues around the country to find the best non-Hodgkin lymphoma specialist in the country. After some calls he found that one name kept popping up, Dr. Sandra Horning, who was a world expert in the disease. And she worked at Stanford Cancer Clinic, only an hour from my home.

Similarly Dave suggested that I get a second opinion. He mentioned that I should run the idea by my present oncologist as a courtesy. I talked it over with him at my next appointment.

I asked my oncologist if there is any treatment which offered a cure. He replied that it was too late for an experimental treatment which was the only chance for a "cure" because I had already started chemotherapy. We had briefly discussed the option of experimental treatments before I began chemo but I was so hunkered down in shock that I did not rationally weigh the option of taking a chance on an experimental treatment in hopes of a cure. Furthermore he had flatly stated in that earlier conversation that cure was not even an option so I did not realize that an experimental procedure offered a cure. Now he told me that such an option's availability had passed. But then he reiterated that cure was not possible which confused me, not for the first or last time.

"Well, are you comfortable with my diagnosis because if not, I can get a second opinion and further review my options?" I responded.

He retorted, "There is no 'cure 'at Stanford. One doctor there had some success re-treating some lymphoma patients with their own antibodies. But the statistics showed that the long-term result was no better than if the patients had regular chemotherapy, and the procedure cost $300,000. I'm secure with your diagnosis. Since 1970 there have been no changes in the treatment of patients with low grade NHL [non-Hodgkin lymphoma] like yours. Therefore, your treatment is clear."

"It's not worth my visiting a doctor at Stanford . . . ?"

"If you went to Stanford they would list a bunch of options, none any more useful than what I have prescribed. I am very comfortable with your treatment. Your disease will become more like a chronic disease than an acute disease."

My courtesy conversation with him talked me out of Paul's and Dave's advice. I waddled forward and hoped for the best.

Two months later my oncologist started me on the experimental drug which he had mentioned earlier, Rituximab. I was placed in yet another room in his office which at least this time had a view of the street. After setting up the administration of the drug a nurse left the room after warning me to call her I began to itch which could mean that I was having an adverse reaction. Slowly I noticed that my scalp and then my chest started to itch a bit and then more. Since it was subtle for a while I thought it was only my imagination.

But it continued to worsen so I called in the nurse. By now I was having difficulty breathing through my nose and finally stopped breathing through it altogether. Then the back of my throat started to itch as my chest tightened. These symptoms revealed that I soon would suffer from anaphylactic shock which would stop my breathing altogether!

Alarmed the nurse took a bag of Benadryl which would stop the allergic reaction out of the cabinet. But she did not have the authority to give it to me. She alerted the oncologist but he unfortunately was with another patient. Her urgent requests could not drag him away. Meanwhile I kept getting worse.

At long last he casually walked into my room and set up the Benadryl. Little by little the symptoms abated. He cut short the administration of the Rituximab, mumbling that the next time he gave it to me he would pretreat me with Benadryl.

After the Benedryl episode I went home and called Paul who reiterated Dave's suggestion for a second opinion, meaning I should try to visit Dr. Horning. At my next appointment with my oncologist I again asked if I should get a second opinion. "Well, your lymph nodes have not shrunk completely which I had expected. We will do two or three more rounds of chemo and then stop. Stanford is the number one lymphoma center in the world. I have sent people for second opinions there all the time. But I do not need to send you. You do not have that much lymphoma in your body."

Again he was downplaying any need for a trip to Stanford while in the same breath admitting that it provided the best care for lymphoma patients on the planet which I had not known until this point.

Two days later Paul called.

"I talked with a lymphoma specialist at Yale University who suggested a sibling bone marrow transplant for you. It poses no risk for the sibling and would take you a year to recover. But it would cure you! **Cure has a nice ring to it, doesn't it?** There is risk because it kills off your immune system first before your body can accept your sibling's bone marrow. The specialist likes to do it early in the life of the lymphoma progression meaning now. That is because after the lymphoma returns a couple of times it becomes stronger. You need to talk to Dr. Horning at Stanford and ask her if you should switch to her; ask her about your expected life span without the transplant and whether a sibling transplant would work. And your oncologist is right - Stanford is the biggest lymphoma center in the world!"

After hanging up with Paul I resolved to call Stanford to meet with this world famous Dr. Horning. Paul's and Dave's encouragement had swung the balance away from my oncologist's naysaying.

I was put through directly to Dr. Horning's secretary who said that the doctor normally sees patients on Tuesdays. And I could come next Tuesday! Just like that! I now had an appointment with one of the best physicians in the world at the largest treatment center in the world for my particular cancer. I felt a huge surge of relief.

Two days later I called my oncologist to inform him that I would see Dr. Horning. He responded, "I do not recommend transplants because the chances of cure are slim. I had several patients do transplants in the 80s and 90s which caused serious and chronic GI tract problems or the transplants did not even work. Let's not forget that they can kill you. Yale pushes them because that's what they do - research and learn from these procedures. Your longevity is eight to ten years."

He continued, "Your anxiety about all this will pass in about six months when you feel better. It is good that you go to Stanford to hear this from a second source. But they will publicize any new cancer treatment in the local newspaper. Transplants are not a cure because they do not get all the cancer. The bottom line is that you have a disease which we cannot control; low-grade non-Hodgkin lymphoma is not manageable beyond a certain point and you will have to live with that answer today."

Somebody was wrong. Yale said it could cure me. My oncologist's transplant experiences occurred decades before. Transplant methodology continued to improve. If Stanford was the best place to get treatment for lymphoma perhaps it would know more about the latest therapies than that in the newspaper. And suddenly it was "good" that I get a second opinion. I was growing suspicious of my present oncologist's ability to meet my medical needs although I did not recognize it yet.

Then I met the highly recommended Dr. Sandra Horning. "She's a world expert," kept ringing in my ears. My expectations and hopes ran very high when she entered the patient room. After I met her I relaxed. She was very warm and friendly. She answered my questions honestly and informatively. I got the clear impression that I was seeing only the tip of the massive iceberg below the surface of her vast intelligence and knowledge. I knew that she was an expert. I knew that I had found my sanctuary from the tempest of my cancer's storm.

She informed me that, "You need to stop chemotherapy right now. You have had 11 doses when six is the appropriate amount. Chemo for you is like a binge and a poisonous one. And chemotherapy does not do that much to stop it anyway. Lymphoma just *is*. From what I see I would not recommend a transplant at this time but I will reconsider it later. Do not do your own research on the internet but talk to me instead."

She countered everything my oncologist had said and done. But I still was emotionally reeling from my surprise diagnosis, powerful medications, and conflicting opinions. Therefore I continued to stumble along not sure where I was going.

When I returned to my oncologist with Dr. Horning's information he immediately agreed to stop the chemotherapy. He said that I would not need further treatment for at least four months. Also he said that going to Dr. Horning would serve the purpose of staying updated on the latest research rather than finding it in the newspapers or causing me confusion as he had argued earlier.

Then two weeks later like a clear sign from heaven, my left hip swelled for no apparent reason. I visited my original oncologist who concluded that the lymph nodes were draining into the hip area because my bone marrow was full of lymphoma. He prescribed a steroid to stop the swelling. After taking the steroid the swelling receded immediately.

I had already scheduled a second appointment with Dr. Horning so I discussed the hip swelling with her. She informed me that the swelling had nothing to do with my lymphoma. It had gone up and down in size much too fast to be lymphoma.

"You need to switch oncologists!" exclaimed Dave in our phone conversation following my appointment with Dr. Horning. "You don't know it but you have already lost confidence in your first oncologist. He blatantly misdiagnosed the bump on your hip. You've had too many problems along the way with his treatment plan which was not supported by Dr. Horning. You definitely need to switch to Dr. Horning. She is a world expert in non-Hodgkin lymphoma and Stanford is not that far away. Pick up the phone and call Dr. Horning. Get it over with."

I balked because I thought she saw Presidents and such. Dave quickly allayed those concerns, "What do you think she does all day? Sees people like you! She is a doctor who sees everyone, just like I do." That was good enough for me.

I called and switched my care to her right then. Her secretary told me the wonderful news that she had room for me. I now had perhaps the best non-Hodgkin lymphoma specialist in the world as my oncologist!

I had to explain to my first oncologist that I was leaving him. In our phone conversation he graciously offered, "You have to be sure about your care."

At my next appointment with my new oncologist, Dr. Horning, she raised my hopes even higher by saying that, "Many changes in the form of new treatments can happen in just two years. Your prognosis is for ten years which bodes well for many changes to arise in the meantime."

Now against my impossible diagnosis of terminal cancer stood the possibility of miraculous healing which I had witnessed firsthand in my hometown along with the fantastic news that my personal oncologist was a world expert in my particular form of cancer! The impossibility of my diagnosis was not as impossible as it first seemed.

CHAPTER 11

Rita

After a four-month sabbatical I returned to work at my church during the summer of 1999. It felt good to get back to my office and responsibilities. My cardiologist friend Dave informed me that, "Work is good for you; it provides eu[good]stress rather than distress. Not working at all can cause more stress than a reasonable amount of work." But I needed to pace myself. As my original oncologist had instructed me, "If you put in a full day at church, take a day off to recover. Half on and half off." He was right. My illness caused significant fatigue.

As a pastor in a small church I had to carry spiritual and emotional loads of those who came to my church. Some people wanted my full attention even when it was not available. One member even wanted my personal phone number so she could call me whenever she had a headache. Fortunately one of the church leaders heard about it and talked her out of it.

The interim pastor Diana who had taken over in my absence was a very pleasant and warm person. I asked her to take charge of visiting people and emotionally supporting the members while I handled the more formal administrative and leadership roles which included preaching.

Thankfully the members of my church were extremely kindhearted. They gave me plenty of space allowing me to settle in comfortably. I was returning home to a *family* rather than to a job.

A few months later I had enough energy to drive two hours to the final lunch at an annual pastor conference. I sat down at a table which included the wife of a minister whom I had been wanting to meet for over 20 years. The uncle who had persuaded me to attend the healing conference at his Glendale church often had raved about one of his pastors Bob Whitaker. Now his wife sat across from me at the table.

I told her about how my uncle wanted me to meet her husband, "Well, he is sitting right behind you!" she rejoined. After lunch I finally met him. I learned that his wife and he had served as prayer counselors at the retreat. His exhaustion let me know how many hours they had spent providing insight and guidance to the pastors.

Despite their tiredness I did not want to let another special opportunity for some prayer to pass me by. They kindly agreed to meet me in an hour in the chapel.

I arrived in the empty, dark chapel before they did. In the small empty building near the large, stained glass window I waited expectantly. After they arrived they immediately began to pray over me. They told me things about myself that were personal and which they could not have known beforehand. Clearly they both had a gift of discernment. Specifically they recognized my complex and painful relationship with my father.

After the prayer time Bob strongly encouraged me to go to an emotional healing conference offered every summer in Edmonds, Washington by its founder Rita Bennett. She was the widow of an Episcopalian priest who had sparked the inclusion of supernatural gifts into the Episcopal Church in America in the 1970s. Normally I would have ignored the whole idea. However I viewed life differently now which meant that I listened to more far-fetched suggestions. I went to places and events that I would not have considered before. I would need to go to the unusual to obtain the unusual.

A few months later in the summer of 2000 I arrived in the packed meeting room in the hotel in Edmonds, Washington.

I immediately liked Rita. She radiated a vibrant faith and enthusiasm. Upon meeting her and then watching her lead the seminar during the first day I could not help but absorb some of her joy. Her continual mood of expectation that God would help us and heal us permeated my spirit. I grew more hopeful by the day.

Rita appeared as a beautiful, effervescent woman whose love touched deeply inside of me. I felt absolutely accepted by her. She re-ignited my child's hope for wonderful things to happen. Her hope was contagious and made me genuinely hopeful that healing would come to pass.

Also she conveyed a sense of access to immense spiritual power. Her speech and demeanor not only emanated the likelihood that God could perform miracles but also that God's strength would accomplish *my* needed miracle. It created a dynamic and exciting combination.

Her curriculum taught how emotional healing worked. I knew about counseling and therapy but not emotional healing, especially spiritual. I understood that time spent with a trained therapist could lead someone to understand their psychological make-up which could enhance healthy self-understanding. I did not know that God's Spirit could directly intervene and lead to emotional healing. The conference opened a new window for me into how to find and facilitate healing.

In the evenings Rita hung around with us. We moved the chairs and tables back so we could navigate and sit comfortably. We gathered in groups to pray for each other. In the meantime Rita moved from person to person laying her hands on their heads and shoulders. With her charming smile and benevolent touch she prayed words of encouragement and love into each of us.

When it was my turn she prayed for God's love to break into my spirit and move aside any depression I may have developed from my diagnosis. She perceptibly infused me with the Spirit; I caught in a new and profound way the essence of hoping in the Lord.

She intoned her tender, urgent prayer.

"Lord Jesus, I ask You to bless Don with an outpouring of Your love. Let him know how highly You think of him and how much You want to bring him life. Let him ignore this difficult diagnosis and instead focus on You with Your love and Your power to overcome any depression he may feel. Increase his hope in You. Let him know that You came to overcome death and heal us. You are a loving God. Take care of Don. I pray this in the powerful Name of Your Son Jesus! Amen."

I felt warm, loved, and alive. Her words of hope settled into me. My trust in God's desire and ability to heal me rose astronomically. Once again my faith in His miraculous power to heal me took root.

In the meantime a question arose. Before I came to the conference I had learned that Benny Hinn was returning to the Bay Area but on the same week as Rita's conference. He was coming to San Jose instead of Oakland. San Jose necessitated an hour longer drive from my home so I would need to stay in a hotel as I would not have the energy to drive home after the evening meeting. However San Jose hotels were full because of several conferences during the same week. I could not find a hotel any closer than half the distance from my home which was still too far to drive.

Apparently the circumstances were not lining up for me to see him despite my great interest. He would arrive during the latter part of the week on the exact days as the second half of Rita's conference. I considered attending only the first half of her conference and then flying back for his conference. However I still could not solve the hotel problem.

As the first half of Rita's conference came to a close I had to decide. Everything seemed to line up for me to stay on. I found the conference to provide great encouragement while I could not even find a place to stay near Benny's.

On that last evening of the first half of her conference I wandered into the hall of the hotel and found two other conferees talking. They were both planning to stay on for the second half. I told them of my dilemma. To my astonishment both of them had personal stories involving Benny Hinn. One of them had gone to great effort to visit one of his services after he had injured his knee so badly that he could no longer perform his carpentry work. By the end of the service he walked out the door with his knee completely healed. He returned to work on the following Monday.

The other man who happened to be a teacher at Rita's conference told me that his wife's cousin had been diagnosed with Lou Gehrig's disease (amyotrophic lateral sclerosis) which would be fatal. She was driven to a Benny Hinn crusade and carried to her seat where she suddenly felt led to stand which she did for 20 minutes with her back bent dramatically backwards. Then she started walking down the stairs and ended up running down a hallway. Her healing had begun. Three months later she could wear high heels because the disease had disappeared. She had the medical records to prove it.

I was so blown away by these coincidences I knew that I did not need to go to Benny's conference; rather God could do something special for me wherever I was including at Rita's conference. It confirmed in my mind that the extraordinary events which I had witnessed at Benny's conference in Oakland had happened. Also I noticed that the momentum of my courage to believe in the healing of my cancer again ballooned at that moment.

I ended up seeing Benny Hinn a year later. He came to a San Francisco hotel for three days where three thousand of us stayed and saw him on stage several times a day. On the last day he had everyone come forward in a long line so he could lay his hands on each of us individually. I had the blessing of this powerful, well-known healer as he laid his hands on my head. I could feel God's Spirit move through me which stayed with me for quite a while. I was not totally healed then but it again deepened my trust in the certainty of my eventual healing.

The rest of the week at Rita's conference included many accounts of emotional and physical healing. Rita prayed for me personally again which gave me more encouragement and a greater sense of God's Spirit moving in me. I went home with a freer sense of my relationship with God along with a greater enthusiasm about pursuing healing for my cancer. Cure indeed had a nice ring to it.

Her zeal to push through the barriers of disbelief and fear to achieve a miracle impressed me. Not only could I hope for healing I could actively seek it. My experience of God did not have to stay placid and passive. Instead it could take on a more proactive approach.

Since I normally co-partnered with God in making less important day-to-day decisions I should have a direct role in pursuing my healing rather than merely waiting for God to do a miracle for me.

Scripture had many places where people sought help from God to fix their desperate circumstances and God came through. People did not have to accept things as they were and do nothing. King Hezekiah turned to God in II Kings 18 to save his kingdom from a more powerful attacking king and God saved it. I could seek God doing a miracle for me as could anyone.

CHAPTER 12

Healing Genes

My dad once told me he recalled sitting on his doorstep as a boy and asked a neighbor how someone could become President of the United States. He always set his goals high and he had the drive and energy to reach them.

He needed 21 merit badges to become an Eagle Scout so he got 39 of them. He became Student Body President of his high school, played in the orchestra, took part in sports, joined several clubs, and graduated early. In college he paid his way by forming a dance band which eventually morphed into six bands that brought in so much money he bought a new sports car and stayed an extra year in college because he could not afford to graduate.

When the people at a meeting in Oakland concluded that they could not successfully pass a school bond measure after several attempts had failed he stood up in the back of the auditorium and said they could! They made him chairman of the committee which successfully got the bond passed in the next election. This effort led to his election as a State Assemblyman.

As a man who worked for him recently told me, "He was a fighter!"

Perhaps this energy was the source of my immediate interest in finding healing. I could not accept that God could not fix my cancer problem. It made no sense to me that cancer had to win. God is bigger than anything including a terminal disease. I innately knew He could cure me. So I actively sought it out.

On the other hand my mother had a very understated, placid spirit along with a quiet and strong faith in God. To her life was okay. She did not talk about her faith; she implied it.

I knew that she trusted in a loving God especially when she would look at me with a knowing twinkle in her eye whenever I talked about God. She carried a warm, gentle glow like Donna Reed in the well-known Christmas movie *It's a Wonderful Life!* She did not tell me of God's loving faithfulness; she was God's faithfulness. I absorbed her example which blessed me.

When I was six she sent me off to a Vacation Bible School for two weeks during the summer. I could walk to the church which sat next to the original Dreyer's Ice Cream Shop in Oakland.

Some very sweet teachers explained God to us, that God was full of lovingkindness like the perfect grandparent. God wanted to know us so much that He became a human being, Jesus. Jesus was very popular because He could answer the questions of life, was very warm and caring, and even did miracles. Lots of miracles.

Then He died a terrible death which somehow made a way for us to get to heaven. He returned to life and eventually went to heaven. Soon He returned to earth in the form of His essence, His Spirit. And we could include that Spirit into our lives if we wanted which meant that we could experience what He did, such as the love of God, power in our spirits, and ability to receive miracles.

I liked the whole idea so I asked this Spirit into my spirit. This unseen presence of love and constancy would sustain me throughout my life. Like my mother's knowing faith, my own faith would never fail me as it grew, matured, and transformed. She had given me a most precious gift, that of finding and knowing God personally for my whole life.

I never talked with her about how she handled stress. She wore it like a shawl with her head held high. Her life was not easy. When problems came to the door, she bore up with grace. I tried to copy her sense of calm when cancer came to my door.

During the first few years of my cancer I lost them both. My grief ran deeply within me but their spirits blazed up to sustain me as my years with cancer progressed.

CHAPTER 13

Return to Life?

How am I feeling today?

Are any alarms going off somewhere in my body?

Wow, I feel tired, chemo tired.

Thoughts like these became part of my daily internal conversation. When someone asked me how I was doing I needed several seconds to figure out my answer. I lived in the alternative world of chemicals and disease. I aimed my life force inward to focus my energy on doing all that I could to get well. I had no choice.

Slowly I emerged from my self-imposed social timeout to return to my community. I had to do it in stages. I noticed that although I thought I was fully present when talking with someone I would then catch my reflection in a pane of glass or a mirror and see this wooden man talking unemotionally with that person. Who was that man in the mirror?

At the same time I realized how much my family and friends loved me. They knew that I was in a fix, fighting to get over this terminal disease while attempting to connect with them. They waited patiently as I slowly returned to their world.

A friend called to invite me to a book/dinner club that met every two weeks. I readily accepted even though I had to drive for over an hour each way to Menlo Park to attend. It proved worthwhile. Seven of us unmarried men and women feasted and laughed as we shared stories and discussed books about relationships. I always left those repasts feeling more like a normal person.

Fortunately I received several lunch and dinner invitations always with the freedom to change my mind at the last minute. One time after my close friend had flown in from Colorado to see a play with me I had to tell him when he arrived at my door I was too tired and sick to accompany him. He characteristically took it in stride.

And thankfully I was able to officiate two of my nieces' weddings. My eldest niece Emily, my sister Donna's eldest daughter, was the first to get married of all my nieces and nephews. I performed her wedding along with Bob Barram, the associate pastor at her home church, Piedmont Community. Bob had been my Young Life youth ministry leader when I was in high school. Now we got to marry Emily together. It turned out that Bob led the service using the wedding liturgy while I ad-libbed with jokes. Emily and Shawn loved it all as did our family and friends.

Years later I did it again, this time performing the marriage of my other sister Patty's oldest child Diana. Because I was weaker by then, I played a more limited role. I still had the wonderful opportunity to lead them through their vows. The wedding was held at Diana's father's family's property where he had married my sister. After the wedding a family friend who had grown up a few doors down from me said how my voice leading Patty's daughter through her vows made the ceremony "complete."

Other occasional serendipities would remind me I had many who cared for me.

One day Patty's brother-in-law Bill called out of the blue to say that he was praying for me since my name came to his mind during his prayers that morning.

On another day when my body and emotions seemed in complete rebellion I had four calls in a row from folks who encouraged me, ending with an invitation to get together the next day. On another uncomfortable day when I could not calm myself a musician friend dropped by and took me out to buy me a guitar.

My anger rarely broke out probably because of my personality as well as my mother's influence. Also my medications included something that calmed my nerves. Usually I felt peaceful albeit tired. But the anger was there. After all, I kept being told that I would die. However God's love in my spirit, the reaching out by those who loved me, and the occasional rays of hope from a healing teaching or miracle all mitigated against my anger. Whenever I exploded it did not comprise more than briefly yelling.

I found that I could yell at God in my journal. I could throw temper tantrums in a constructive way such as:

I feel trapped! . . . But then God regrew the people of Israel from nearly nothing. I guess I'm not trapped after all.

Around this time my cardiologist friend Dave along with his wife Chris threw me a birthday party. During the party he took a moment to say some kind words about me to our friends which meant a great deal to me. The following morning we went together to First Presbyterian Church Berkeley where one pastor Tim Shaw, who had been a roommate of mine some years previously, took a moment in the service to honor me. These moments comforted and strengthened me

These serendipities brightened the grinding journey of serving as a part-time pastor with a limited personal life, who otherwise battled cancer. And on it went for a few years.

I still could preach along with my other duties which brought me joy. I maintained a social life. And I slept a lot.

CHAPTER 14

Second Round

Finally Dr. Horning decided that I needed to start a second round of chemotherapy. I had been leading the church for almost four years since my diagnosis. The church had witnessed me going through so many changes as I preached every Sunday. Now I would have to drive to Stanford for treatments and go through more changes, physically and emotionally, which the church would witness every Sunday morning when I preached. I had reached the end of my strength for this role.

As I came to this difficult realization, I concluded that I had to leave the church. Yet I felt relief. I had gone through enough. And I could move closer to the Stanford Cancer Clinic which would eliminate the long drives for appointments and treatments. It was the right time.

In 2003 I announced my difficult decision to the leadership committee the Session. They understood and sorrowed with me. They gave me a moving and touching farewell reception with guest speakers. For such a caring *family* I felt like I had hardly gotten to know them because of the distraction of my illness. Now we were saying goodbye. I felt so loved and so sad to lose connection with them..

I moved to Menlo Park, two miles from the Cancer Clinic. Cardiologist Dave was not so sure that I should relocate farther away from him. He wanted to monitor my condition and was afraid that I would find myself alone which would lead to depression. But I wanted to regain more control over my situation. I did not want my Stanford oncologist so far away.

I found a nice apartment complex across from an elementary school on a quiet street. It had a good-sized pool placed under attractive palm trees. And unlike my last apartment complex the neighbors were friendly. We even had parties on Saturday nights which always were fun.

One couple Tarny and Tess regularly invited me over to pray for my healing. Other neighbors like Mike and Lee often checked up on me. Another neighbor who was a high school English teacher continually engaged me in long conversations about Shakespeare which I found fascinating. Once another friend from the apartment complex told me she awoke in the middle of the night to pray for me.

Also the move meant that I would live near Menlo Park Presbyterian Church where I had worked as an intern for several years. Thousands of people attended the church every Sunday so plenty of support was available for me.

Within a week of moving I went to a service and ran into an old friend who was forming a new men's group. Bill was a natural leader around whom men habitually gathered. He welcomed me into the group of six other strong, friendly men who buoyed me up during the rough years ahead.

We met every two weeks at a different home of one of these men. The host provided the entrée while the rest of us brought other dishes. I never ate that well in my life. It was not hot dogs and pizza; it was pot roast and spare ribs.

After chatting over dinner we would move to the living room to discuss some topic which we had studied ahead of time. We would close our meetings with prayers about family, health, and other issues. This covering of prayer and depth of friendship meant a great deal to me.

The guys would help me out in other ways often volunteering to walk with me for exercise. I believe that the group provided one reason that I ultimately survived.

Occasionally other groups at Menlo Park Presbyterian Church would pray for me.

My difficult decision to leave my church and Richmond turned out to be the right one.

CHAPTER 15

The Basement

I should have known what was in store when the receptionist told me to find the cancer clinic in the basement of Stanford Hospital. Hospitals are like airports with huge sets of buildings littered with confusing signs. They should provide guides who lead tours of all the alcoves and hallways with explanations of what door signs with large triangles and exclamation points mean. Stanford Hospital was no exception. (Since this time, it has opened a new, more updated hospital.)

To enter the basement with steam pipes and roughed textured walls did not allay my anxiety about receiving more chemo in the basement. As I descended the narrow escalator next to the gift shop I did not miss the irony of leaving the bright space full of flowers and gifts to enter the bowels of the hospital to receive more poison.

When I arrived at the tiny infusion center in the basement for the first time I felt like I had joined part of a MASH unit from a war zone. Long, aging recliners and narrow stretchers serving as makeshift beds crammed the stuffy, unventilated room. Poles holding up bags of drugs punctuated the whole room. Cancer patients in various stages of decline fully occupied all the furniture. Amid all this nurses and aides stepped gingerly stepped over and around the patients.

A smiling nurse led to my assigned recliner. As I stretched out my frame onto the slightly off-balance leathery chair I tried to relax. I pulled on the lever to lift the leg support which came up with a muttered groan and locked into place albeit at a slight angle. I looked around the room and took in the apparent confusion.

The televisions dotting the walls added to the low-level chaos by trumpeting game shows, like *Who Wants to Be a Millionaire?* or *Family Feud*, along with several soap operas.

Half walls split up the small room into even smaller areas. The bottoms of the recliner chairs faced toward the center of a walled off section so patients could look at each other - or not. This sometimes led to some interesting conversations about our respective cancer experiences which engendered an esprit de corps among us.

We were all gathered together virtually one on top of another soldiering through the same challenges. This brought out a camaraderie which even included the staff. The nurses and aides appeared to thrive on the friendly intensity of the situation and exuded a brightness which helped turn the drudgery into more of a carnival. It was almost fun.

We even had a visiting clown who tried to cheer us up with corny jokes.

There were some exceptions to the frivolous spirits. Once a young man sitting next to me intently focused on his several business magazines while his ignored wife sat dutifully next to him. The man curtly told me he was only allowing the cancer to use up three months of his valuable time. That was it. Godspeed young man.

When it was my turn I laid my left arm on the armrest so the nurse could start my infusion. First she wrapped my lower arm in a hot towel to facilitate the veins rising to the surface. Effective infusion is all about a *good stick.*

The nurse wanted to poke the needle from the tubing into a vein seamlessly and painlessly. Sometimes that happened. However usually the needle would hit one of the many flaps in the vein which move the blood flow along. I knew it when she hit a flap; it hurt! She securely taped the attached tubing thoroughly and tightly to my arm after successfully inserting the needle.

As the drugs entered my arm they always made me sleepy so the time passed dreamily. I brought books to read but rarely looked at them. I reclined in a semi-pleasant stupor. It became my monastic time. Some people go to monasteries for silence to be with God. I found God as I lay reclining in those chairs drifting into a haze as the drugs coursed through me for a few hours.

There was talk in the infusion center of a new cancer clinic opening eventually but its opening surprised me nonetheless. These crowding problems evaporated. Brand-new, well-balanced recliner chairs sat a comfortable distance from each other. Each patient could even pull a curtain around his or her chair for privacy. Each chair had its own small TV/Media center on the long arm extending from the wall!

The new infusion center sat on the second floor of the new cancer clinic building which allowed patients to look out wall-to-ceiling windows onto the beautiful, tall redwood trees below. Rather than one crammed room the infusion center offered several large rooms of recliners along with many private bedrooms for patients to lie down.

This wonderful new center lacked only one thing - intimacy. The nurses were still friendly but the patients were less inclined to talk with each other. The distance from one another ended the sense of camaraderie. We sat alone in our silence. However nothing is perfect. Actually the newly found solitude allowed for the rest we so badly needed. If a patient wanted to talk he or she could bring someone for company.

CHAPTER 16

Concoctions

"People will approach you with their favorite cure for cancer -
some kind of homemade concoction or special juice or powder with
hidden healing qualities. You must learn how to deter them and not
take them."

My first oncologist had warned me that well-meaning people
would offer me secret cures for my cancer. He was right.

One of my friends offered me her special healing juice. She told
me that the juice came from an unknown Pacific island. It contained
untested ingredients that could cure diseases like cancer. She said that
I could get it directly from her. I never got around to asking her for it
but saw this same juice on a shelf at a nearby organic food store. I
bought a gallon of the stuff.

I kept it in my refrigerator and took a swig every morning which
then drove me to the mouthwash because of the terrible taste. I
faithfully kept swigging it until I finished. I felt no different and got
no better.

One day I saw her again.

"You know, I tried it but it didn't help."

"That's because you didn't get it from me!"

Oh . . .

Upon further reflection it made no sense to me that I had to go to
some friend or down some back alley to knock on a garage door and
ask for *Al* to find a cure for cancer.

Some other well-meaning people told me that juicing, mashing up
fruit and vegetables to make a drink, would cure my cancer. I went

out and bought a large, expensive juicing machine. For weeks I drank my way through pounds of fruit and vegetables. The mixture of all the ingredients left a bitter taste. I did not get any better but I did get tired. The mashing, mixing, and grinding took a lot of time to set up and more time to clean up. Eventually I just watched TV instead.

Another friend who was suffering from cancer swore by vitamin B-12 injections. She pointed me toward her *provider* so I went to pay him a visit. His office was actually an apartment in a large building.

He invited me to lay on the table after taking off my shirt. He then taped six little electrical buttons on my chest much like the procedure for an EKG. The buttons connected to wires that ran to some small machine that looked remarkably like an old tape recorder. He turned on the motor and I lay there for 20 minutes with the machine humming along next to me.

When the test ended the machine produced a paper which had some squiggly lines on it. He explained that the readings showed that I would benefit from a vitamin B-12 boost. I put my shirt back on and we moved to another part of his office. I thought this would be a good moment to ask some questions.

"Where did you get your training?"

"I was trained as a sports physical therapist in the South."

"What brought you to California?"

"My license expired, and I moved here."

"Are you licensed here?"

"No . . . Well I think that's enough conversation. Why don't I get you your B-12 shot?"

"You know I don't think I want a shot today."

He looked aghast.

"Are you sure . . . ?"

"Yes, I am. But thank you very much for your time. Here's your $500."

We shook hands and I walked out the door.

These interludes came along with the cancer experience. Juicing was still healthy even though not curative. If I was going to explore various solutions, the exploration was going to be *interesting*.

CHAPTER 17

Much Ado About Nothing

But there is always more . . . After I had moved to Menlo Park and started receiving treatment at Stanford problems arose.

Unexplained swelling in my right eye led my eye doctor to arrange for an immediate operation to sever the artery to the right eye before an impingement on the nerve or I could go immediately blind in that eye. Some kind of inflammation caused this swelling in my head. He did not know why. I had the operation within a few days.

Doctor Horning said that cancer did not cause the inflammation and she did not know what the eye problem was about. Her physician assistant informed me my sed rate which determines the amount of inflammation in the body was high.

The next day, I visited my internal medicine doctor because I could not walk because of left knee pain. She sent me to a rheumatologist who did not agree that inflammation caused the eye swelling.

Then on the next day Dr. Horning told me that, "You have an autoimmune problem: your immune system is attacking rather than protecting healthy tissue. This is not common with non-Hodgkin lymphoma. Your case is uncommon. As for the inflammation problem I have no answers."

Each new day brought a new speculative diagnosis. I felt whipsawed by multiple opinions. Many more appointments followed.

I visited a dermatologist who agreed that I had inflammation but had no answers. My rheumatologist discovered a protein in my blood called monoclonal IgM kappa which could have caused the inflammation. Meanwhile my internal medicine doctor found a mass on my lung which fortunately turned out to be a non-malignant calcified node. But within a day or two my internal medicine doctor told me that my head and eye lid were swelling. Also she found pseudo-gout. The next day my ophthalmologist told me that my eye was okay.

A few days later my rheumatologist said that perhaps I had a very rare disease of angio (vascular) edema (swelling) because of the swelling in my face. This meant that the lymphoma must be the cause. She sent me to an allergist who was very concerned that if my facial swelling continued it could close my airways.

Next Dr. Horning concluded, "Your case is unusual; you have low platelets and some stomach issues along with your new inflammation issue. I have never seen inflammation in one of my patients in over 20 years of practice when the cancer is declining. Maybe your spontaneous regression tripped off your body's balance so it is unable to stop the inflammation."

However later that day the rheumatologist called with the good news that the test for the angio-edema was negative. Two days later my new neurologist told me that my sed rate was the highest he had ever seen!

Two weeks later Dr. Horning's nurse practitioner called to say that the latest MRI led the Stanford neurology and radiation departments to agree with Dr. Horning that I had some kind of tumor in my brain. But it was not an emergency since I felt no symptoms. I never knew that a brain tumor was not an emergency.

Nonetheless I had a spinal tap to learn more about it.

When I saw Dr. Horning she continued to be surprised.

"I have never seen a case like yours! Your blood is excellent and the CAT scan was fine. Non-Hodgkin lymphoma rarely causes inflammation although some other cancers do. It could just be inflammation."

The nurse practitioner called later to say that the spinal tap showed that I had no lymphoma in my brain fluid. I did not have a brain tumor after all.

Then another allergist thought I might have a low protein C1 but a test ended that idea. She sent me to the Chair of Rheumatology at the University of California, San Francisco, who specialized in strange cases like mine. He told me I did not have a problem.

"You have no tumor or bone marrow issue. If you had a protein issue it was not an allergy because you are not itching."

Finally Dr. Horning told me that my painful knee inflammation was indeed a lymphoma issue.

"Your latest MRI showed that lymphoma is everywhere so all these other theories probably were much ado about nothing. Your cancer is present but need not receive treatment at this point. For now since the symptoms were all caused by your cancer which is essentially under control you don't have to do anything."

In the middle of this chaos Dr. Horning switched my neurologist to one who specialized in cancer neurology. We met in his Stanford office. Dr. Larry Recht immediately commented on my disposition.

"You are unlike my other patients. You seem relaxed, centered with all this. You remind me of an Episcopal priest whom I knew in Worcester, Massachusetts. He was a nice guy, just himself."

My cardiologist friend Dave had advised me early on, "Do everything the doctors tell you and seek God's help in any way that you want." I guess it was paying off.

CHAPTER 18

Heaven On Earth

Over the whole course of my illness I fortuitously received the gift of a great many others 'efforts to intercede with God on my behalf.

Incredibly several people lit candles and performed other rituals for me in major spiritual centers around the world.

A seminary classmate said that he had lit a candle for me at the Santa Maria sopra Minerva in Rome, Italy where Catherine of Siena is buried. Catherine was hugely influential in the Middle Ages; her main interest was our intimate union with God which in this life could only be experienced mystically. It reminded me of feeling Jesus 'arms around me every night as I went to sleep.

One man from my small group lit a candle for me at Lourdes, France where in the mid-nineteenth century a young peasant girl saw the Virgin Mary who told her to dig in a certain spot and to drink from the small spring of water that bubbled up. Almost immediately cures from drinking the water occurred. Yet in the modern era the waters there have not shown any special curative properties. Today thousands of gallons of water gush from the source of the spring so pilgrims can bathe in it. Countless reported cures have happened there ranging from the healing of nervous disorders to the cure of paralysis, blindness, and cancer.

Another friend lit a candle for me at the Vatican the center of the Catholic Christian church.

Someone else placed a small slip of paper with a prayer for me into the Wailing Wall or Western Wall in the City of Jerusalem in Israel; it sits near the site of the Temple destroyed by the Romans. It was there during the time of Jesus and is today the holiest site for Jews. It also was and still is a very important site for Muslims as part of Mohammed's pilgrimage. And it is a major Christian pilgrimage site where Christians gather to pray as Jerusalem was where Jesus was crucified, buried, and resurrected. Twice a year, the small prayer notes are collected from the cracks between the massive stones in the Wailing Wall and buried on the Mount of Olives outside of Jerusalem.

My friends traveled to places on earth where God was known to do miracles and asked Him to do one for me. They pursued my healing apart from any effort by me. As I did my part by seeking heavenly intervention into my illness, heavenly intervention was pouring out for me through the care and prayer of my friends.

One evening at our book club dinner group Linda said that her next-door neighbor had invited someone with the gift of healing to come speak in his home. We were all invited to attend. I was still living in Richmond which was an hour away but decided that this could be something that was worthwhile. For three days I travelled to listen to this man teach in great detail about how God physically heals. He explained the theology of healing and told about how he would walk into intensive care units where he prayed for people who then miraculously recovered. He shared about the history of healing rooms in Spokane, Washington which are special rooms where men and women possessing a spiritual gift of healing prayed over people. I learned of healing rooms in the Bay Area so I sought them out and went there.

While I had seen some physical healings I had received little teaching on the subject; Rita's conference had offered instruction more aimed at emotional healing. Listening to stories and explanations about physical healing helped me to accept more easily that physical healings were not surprising or unusual.

I attended a conference offered by Hawaiian Islands Ministries. It met in the Bay Area because its founder came from Menlo Park. Speaker Jordan Seng had a reputation as a healing minister. He had written a book about it, *Miracle Work: A Down-to-Earth Guide to Supernatural Ministries.*

He introduced us to the idea of heaven coming to earth. The principle came from Jesus telling people to repent for, "The kingdom of heaven is at hand." (Matthew 4:17, Mark 1:15) Repent is a very strong word meaning to change radically your understanding, to reverse course. Jesus was trying to inform people that they could accept the powerful idea that now what goes on in heaven can happen on earth. Since heaven had come to earth in the form of Jesus, which was God in physical form, then what goes on in heaven where God is (like no illness) now exists on earth.

Then since Jesus sent Himself in the form of His Spirit to earth, heaven exists on earth today in the presence of His Spirit. Since people are not sick in heaven they do not have to be sick on earth. People's needs get met in heaven so they can get met on earth.

This new teaching helped me be more open-minded. Apparently the Bible said that healing was appropriate and realistic for me. I had not known that the Bible was so clear on the matter and so hopeful. Jesus had healed many but that was so long ago. However His Spirit in the world today acts the same as His presence in the world long ago.

After his teaching Jordan invited anyone who wanted healing to come forward. Several of us gathered around him; after praying a moment he chose me first. As he prayed I felt heat on my face and a sweetness in my spirit.

"You have glory in your bones. A heavy burden is lifted off your shoulders. You are forgiven. God's Spirit is all over you like honey from above," he told me. Glory in my bones sounded helpful since my lymphoma was centered in my bone marrow.

I felt like I did at the Benny Hinn conference. I knew something real was happening. I recognized that the ethereal, warm weightiness swimming around me was God's Spirit Whom I could trust.

As time passed these moments with the Spirit and words of encouragement became cumulative. I increasingly hoped that they would prevail over my cancer. Perhaps my experience with many pastors through the years showed me that each person had a different mix of gifting and power from God. I could accept each prayer experience with gratitude for what happened rather than disappointment from what did not happen. Therefore I did not expect a complete healing from anyone. Each person offered their contribution and I always felt some level of help.

A year later I returned to another gathering at Linda's neighbor's house where I found the world-famous evangelist Luis Palau, who had often worked with Billy Graham. He had brought his brother-in-law, Juan Carlos Ortiz, another well-known pastor. I learned that Juan

Carlos had suffered from cancer so true to form I had to ask him about it.

"God healed me from my melanoma!" he exclaimed.

I told him about my non-Hodgkin lymphoma; he enthusiastically offered to pray for me.

"Jesus, heal this man. And Don, be ready to see Jesus. Walk in joy. Focus on Jesus and not the cancer. Be ready to die. Either is okay."

Juan Carlos 'intense prayer greatly encouraged me. It helped me put my cancer into perspective. I realized again that I trusted God even if I did not get cured. Yet the peace which came from trusting in His continuing presence further assured me that I would survive.

During this time I was attending a monthly healing prayer service held at Menlo Park Presbyterian Church. I joined the healing team leaders 'meetings. These regularly scheduled meetings led to a very close connection among the six of us which overflowed into an ongoing concert of prayer and encouragement for each other.

Two of the members of the group, David and Barbara, had seen many miracles in their own lives. David had received a miraculous healing of severe leg issues which eliminated his need for braces during one of Jordan Seng's conferences. As we continued our prayer times at church David and Barbara saw several people healed through their prayers. The rest of us did as well.

Another leader, Wylie, confidently insisted that God would heal his hearing loss. After years of claiming that God would heal it, it happened! Another leader, a retired Stanford physician, Hudd, fortified us with his perspective on facing the reality of medical threats with a strong faith in God's ability and willingness to heal. Our communal hope kept growing as we faithfully met and prayed so that even from within our little circle God did extraordinary things as people for whom we prayed got answers and sometimes even full healing.

A pastor friend, Carl Hoffman, called on one of my bad days to tell me about his dream from the night before.

"Don, you were standing at Sather Gate [the entry point to the main plaza at the University of California Berkeley, where Carl had gone to college]. I was looking up at you. Your body appeared 'buff 'with a rippling chest like a gladiator. You were a star football player for Cal! You read from the book of Hosea in the Bible."

After we laughed about my rippling chest we bid farewell. I flipped to Hosea where I read in verse 11:8 how God's heart was changed within me arousing all my compassion

Then I turned to Hosea 2:14-15 which said that God was going to give me back my vineyards.

I interpreted all Carl's insights to mean that I would be blessed by God again and restored to full strength. His compassion for me would pour out in due time.

Out of the blue God had moved an old friend to dream a Scripture which would tell me that healing was on the way. These types of miracles happened so often that I concluded that God must be behind them.

I found it incredible that so many supernatural events were not only happening in some distant foreign country but in my town. I could find heaven even where I lived.

CHAPTER 19

Sleeping My Way to Health

A wise, older church member once told me, "Learn to give up figuring it all out. It's okay to sit passively and not deride yourself for doing so. God will work it out." I took her advice to heart. If I felt tired I lay down. Pushing through was out. I planned to sleep my way to health if that is what it took. I figured that my body was already working at a full-time job battling this pernicious disease.

I lived with a tension between conflicting ideas such as Lance Armstrong's overcoming spirit co-existing with a restful spirit. Like Lance I knew that I had my father's warrior spirit which would not accept the defeat of letting the cancer have its way uncontested.

Yet I knew that in my physical condition I could not overpower the cancer. I had to let my body receive what it needed including adequate rest. As my mother had always advised, "Get your rest." Somehow these dueling messages slowly melded into a seamless whole within my psyche as I approached my mix of care-related issues.

My first oncologist went even further when he suggested that, "Denial isn't such a bad thing with cancer. You need a little denial to get through the day." That proved to be true. I had to face my problems but not all the time.

I watched television shows like *The 700 Club* that offered stories of miracles. It daily presented testimonies of real-life healings including those from cancer. I personally had known one woman who had a very serious back issue. She watched this show on a day when they prayed for those with back issues and her back problems ended permanently right then.

Another encouraging episode of the show told of a man who had died in a car accident and returned to life. He claimed that he knew at the moment of the accident that he would return because of the promise in Philippians 1:6 that God had begun a good work in him so would finish the job. On another show I saw a pianist who had suffered from leukemia but received healing. I always felt encouraged after watching these shows.

Sometimes I would spontaneously turn to encouraging verses in the Bible like Psalm 41:3 which told me that God sustains us on our sickbeds and restores us.

Journaling encouraged me as well. I wrote out my thoughts, inspirations, and insights. Philosophical, emotional, and/or theological thoughts often ran through my head. I allowed them out to allow more to come in. The words of hope battled against the feelings of occasional hopelessness on the pages of my journal. There I would sometimes come face to face with my darker side. I would ponder just how is it that God works and exactly where God is during such painful times.

As cardiologist Dave had told me, "Faith is huge for patients. A typical patient wants control but can't have it. One who believes in God has an easier time by passing control of the situation over to God."

CHAPTER 20

Hospital Holiday

I struggled with some dizziness caused by a low blood count. My CAT scans showed normal. Yet other tests showed more lymphoma hidden in my bone marrow. Many nights included thrashing, sweating, leg pain, shortness of breath, and feeling poorly.

Eventually, Dr. Horning started me on a heavy regime of Rituximab. These treatments lasted over several months. After many sessions test data showed that I had improved. "This disease waxes and wanes," my nurse practitioner reminded me.

A seemingly endless run of MRI's proved a constant bother yet necessary as I well understood. The MRI staff would rubber band my feet together and seal my sides with sheets keeping my arms overhead. Then the technicians fitted some kind of contraption over my head to keep my head steady. It had a mirror which at least allowed me to see out the bottom of the tube hopefully to prevent claustrophobia.

Unable to move on the sliding table the staff would move the table into an imposing metallic tube. As the large machine recorded images of the interior of my body it banged loudly. I had to put double ear plugs into each ear to muffle the noise.

While I lay on the sled after sliding into the tube the soothing voice of a technician talked me through the ordeal providing comfort. Then just when I thought it was over they slid me out of the tube to infuse dye into my veins which flushed my body with a warm sensation. Then I was returned back into the tube to finish the examination. It was quite surreal.

My tests showed that something bad was sneaking back.

"Your lymphoma is rare. I will discuss it with our consortium over the next month," Dr. Horning informed me.

I never knew if the rarity of my cancer meant that my chances of healing were better or worse. This uncertainty sustained a continuing low level of anxiety. But my continued spiritual peace served as an effective governor on those feelings.

Finally Dr. Horning decided upon an experimental treatment which could increase the number of cancer killing cells remaining in the part of my immune system not yet affected by the lymphoma. The treatment supposedly had a 50% chance of success.

The next several months did not pass smoothly. Sometimes I had to stop the treatment because of side effects such as lightheadedness and nausea. And sadly it did not even work. My hematocrit (ratio of red blood cells to the rest of the blood cells) score dropped to around half of normal.

By the year's end of 2003 I ended up in the hospital for continuing weight loss. Because they could not determine why that was, they placed a PICC line (soft tube) into my chest to provide nourishment directly into the bloodstream while bypassing the gastrointestinal tract altogether.

Against this harsh news came the joy of a visit by my good friends Jim and Gerri. Since it was Christmastime they had snuck out into the atrium next to my room and strung Christmas lights and decorations on a skinny little tree planted outside my window. They could not bring a Christmas tree into my room because it was not sterile. I felt like Charlie Brown with his skinny scrawny Christmas tree.

Unbeknownst to me they saw my situation as dire because I looked gravely ill. The nurses had given them strict orders to keep their distance from me; they even had to wear face masks and latex gloves. Unaware of these concerns I enjoyed their visit immensely.

Their visit so inspired me with the joy of Christmas that I got up and walked the hospital halls in my Stanford robe and slippers all the while towing my IV pole and passing out CDs of Christmas music from my church. Everyone - staff, patients, and families - gratefully and enthusiastically accepted the CDs. In those moments Christmas came alive for me.

I kept in mind the blessing that my friend Gene had given me a month earlier, "Your illness is for a reason - not just to bless you but also to glorify God. Everything God does is toward that end."

As with most patients in the hospital a team of doctors comprising a seasoned attending oncologist along with several other doctors at various stages of training visited me. One morning that hospital oncologist stated flatly that my symptoms and test results showed that I had stomach cancer; this was a different diagnosis from non-Hodgkin lymphoma.

The hospital oncologist made this announcement as an absolute fact, no question about it. Then the team abruptly walked out. I lay there in bed shocked, confused, and unconvinced of my new diagnosis. During the afternoon I underwent a barium test to confirm her diagnosis. The test came back negative. She was flat out wrong. I knew it!

When the team returned the next morning the oncologist mentioned that the barium test had come back negative.

"So, I don't have stomach cancer?" I probed.

"No, you don't," she admitted embarrassed in front of her team. I glanced at them with their straight faces.

As my cardiologist Dave told me later, "You didn't take bull from anybody!" That was true. Sometimes I became plain angry when I felt mistreated.

Eventually I left the hospital but returned within a week for a transfusion of more platelets. Since the laboratories were full they admitted me back into the hospital for the transfusion.

Next morning I had a visitor from my healing team at church. We were talking casually when Dr. Horning came into my room. The usual gentle and compassionate Dr. Horning gave me a *look* so I asked my friend to leave. Dr. Horning told me the truth straight out.

"Your bone marrow is packed with lymphoma. I am surprised. We will give you four days straight of Rituximab and then one more round of chemotherapy. You need to respond. Your bone marrow is packed. We will put the chemotherapy straight into your PICC line."

I could say nothing but, "OK."

After the intense treatments over the four days she returned to tell me that I needed to go home for a couple weeks and do nothing but rest.

"Things have changed in the last couple of months. It's more perilous now."

"Has the non-Hodgkin lymphoma become aggressive now?"

"It's hard to say," she told me.

Non-Hodgkin lymphoma is a group of blood cancers that includes all types of lymphoma (except Hodgkin) which develops from lymphocytes, a type of white blood cell. Symptoms include enlarged lymph nodes, fever, night sweats, weight loss, and tiredness, all which I experienced at one time or another. Mine was slowly growing (which was common) so that things speeding up meant that it was getting worse.

I left the hospital on Christmas Eve.

Two days later, Dr. Horning told me, "I am encouraged that your platelet count has improved. Your acute platelet episode has passed; your stomach issue was probably nothing more than a long- term virus." The storm had passed - for now.

But Dr. Horning concluded our appointment with the punchline, "It's time to consider a bone marrow transplant."

CHAPTER 21

"Your Transplant Will Not Take Place"

In a later appointment in 2004 Dr. Horning found that the volume of cancer in my bone marrow kept increasing so much that I probably would need a bone marrow transplant very soon. My lymphoma centered in my bone marrow, rather than in the lymph nodes even though my cancer was called *lymph-oma*.

The cancer was flooding my bone marrow. If it completely took it over, 100% of it, I would die. Since she noted that the lymphoma already occupied close to 70% of my marrow I would need the transplant soon.

She concluded with, "We will check your bone marrow before your next visit. If it shows 70% occlusion from the cancer then the transplant is on."

Despite the occlusion or blockage I was still functioning normally. My bones did occasionally feel strange with a perceptible *presence* of something in them. This presence seemed to weaken them, fatigue me, and cause pain. But this phenomenon did not change my activities much unless I got exhausted.

I still had enough energy to track down more people with reputations of manifesting the spiritual gift of physical healing. I had grown to accept that God used certain people to heal supernaturally although I still struggled with the idea that God would use one to heal me. Yet I kept seeking them out.

Two such men, one from Eastern Europe and the other from India, were scheduled to speak together at a conference in Stockton, an hour and a half from my home. I drove there with a friend to a small church in a mall.

I was amazed by how few people came to hear the two reputed healers, fewer than one hundred.

The man from Eastern Europe, who surprisingly was almost blind, spoke of "taking back the land" that we lost in our lives. Isaiah 53:4 states that by the stripes of Jesus we are healed. God allowed Jesus to suffer to undo the losses in our lives.

On the following morning the man from India began relating a very dramatic account of a woman suffering from an illness. Earlier I had told him of my expected bone marrow transplant. Suddenly he interrupted his message and said directly to me, "Don, God just told me that your cancer will leave very soon so your transplant will not take place." Then he continued his talk.

His words stunned and heartened me. Once again I had gone to the effort to travel to receive a healing; maybe I had found it. These repeated moments of *God stuff* where I knew that God was intervening provided huge waves of encouragement. I viewed these attaboys as signs I was on the right track which kept me avidly pursuing healing from both conventional medicine and the power of God's Spirit.

During the evening in Stockton the first man prayed for me. He felt that I had an anointing from God but also that I carried some depression and fear caused by over-analyzing my situation. He believed that I needed the antidote of laughter. He said that he had joy despite his blindness; I guess that explained why God let him remain blind. He conveyed that joy to me.

He prayed that I would have peace and a fresh anointing to hear from God. He encouraged me into an intimacy with Jesus, "Hunger for His Word. Your depression and your fears are generational. This has led to over analyzing by you which has plagued you since your cancer diagnosis. This is why you have difficulty laughing at the moment. Instead you must realize that you are 'clever, 'and can lay hands on the sick and they will be healed."

As I headed home in my car I wondered about the words spoken over me. Would my transplant really be postponed? Would I too pray for people so they would be healed?

I did not resent the words about my being over analytical. I agreed with them because I knew them to be true; that was why I kept long lists of questions for my doctors. But finding laughter in my cancer? That was a tall order.

I did not have my next appointment with Dr. Horning until two months after the Stockton conference. On the night before my appointment I talked with my doctor friends Dave and Paul. We discussed how at the last time that I had seen Dr. Horning my cancer bone marrow involvement had been at a very high 70%. She had told me during that appointment that it had to decrease to a much lower 20% of my bone marrow to cancel the transplant.

Dave wanted to know why improvement in the bone marrow was a condition for not having the transplant. Nevertheless he encouraged me to ignore my feelings and go with her counsel. At that moment I really did not want to go through with the transplant. I wanted so much for the words of prophecy from the Stockton conference to come true.

Meanwhile Paul was curious.

"What is the downside of waiting? If your bone marrow improves then it could get even better without the transplant. How likely is it that your lymphoma will get worse? Most importantly what would she do in these circumstances?"

With trepidation and hope I went to see Dr. Horning. In the examination room Stanford kindly provided laptops for patients. I looked up my emails. I had recently been emailing my friends to pray for me about the transplant. Incredibly the entire front page of 25 headings all referred to my prayer request with words like, "Praying for you!"

Dr. Horning entered the patient room with a confounded look on her face.

"In December your bone marrow had 80% occlusion caused by the cancer. During your February appointment it was 70%. In June it was 60%. Today it is 20%. This is indeed a surprise!"

"Maybe it's from spontaneous remission. I know that it is not due to a lucky poke at your bone marrow biopsy. It's not from your last chemotherapy in February. Also you look much healthier now and your test data are all good. I wonder how these results might have occurred."

She paused reflectively which led me to direct her attention to the laptop screen with the list of people praying for me. She looked at the email list for a moment and then turned back to me with a puzzled look on her face.

Then she continued, "You can postpone the transplant but you probably will not get better. (But that's not impossible and has happened to a few of my patients. One has been cancer free for 16 years.) However if you don't do the transplant the cancer could transmute to something worse. But then again if you do it now you have a 20% chance of dying and a good chance of significant graft versus host disease. So . . . if I were you . . . I'D WAIT! I'm conservative. There're lots of factors in play here and you're doing better at the moment so why not wait?"

It did not take long for me to agree with her to postpone the transplant.

It was an incredible moment. The conference speaker was right! I began jumping up and down inside.

Again the inexplicable had happened - to me.

CHAPTER 22

"Sure."

Amidst all this disarray I went to a dance.

I had not been to one for years. I heard of a singles group hosting one nearby in a barn of all places.

On my way from my car into the dance I ran into Rosie, a woman whom I had known at church years earlier. She recently had received a *word* from the Lord about me even though she had not seen me for years. She did not even know where to find me so put it out of her mind. Then her friend had talked her into going to the dance that evening and here I was!

After sharing a greeting with me she told me her *word* from God for me.

"Give your whole heart to God. Go to Redding to receive prayer from Bill Johnson, the senior pastor at Bethel Church. He specializes in cancer healing. I have a friend whose parents were healed of cancer. And, Don, God likes your prayers of worship on your knees."

Once again an outright miracle had happened. God had reached down to tell me what to do and that everything would turn out all right. Like the pastor who told me to go to Rita Bennett again I was told to travel to a place where I had never been to find healing from a certain person.

I went to Bethel two weeks later with another friend. It was 2005. After the four-hour drive to Redding and a good night's sleep in my hotel I attended the second of Bethel's two services. As I drove into the parking lot I observed a plain, large rectangular building with people streaming in and out of it. I joined the throngs heading in.

As usual my goal was to introduce myself to another person gifted in healing. I entered the large meeting room where I noticed a man toward the back talking casually to a younger man who appeared to be about my age. I guessed that the older man was Bill Johnson. He had dressed in jeans and a button-down shirt with the cuffs turned up. He carried a quiet sense of authority.

When their conversation ended he passed by me so I politely stopped him.

"Excuse me, are you Bill Johnson?"

"Yes I am."

"Good. I'm from out of town. I have cancer. I heard that you pray for people with cancer. I was wondering if you would pray for me after the service?"

"Sure."

As easy as that. No, "Talk to my assistant" or, "I am unavailable." Then he turned and walked down the main aisle to the front of the church. As I watched him do so, another man about my age stepped out from the seats and stopped him. Bill talked to him briefly after which he proceeded to the front of the room.

He immediately started the second service.

"Okay. In the last five minutes three men have come up to me and said, 'Hi. I'm from out of town. I have cancer. Would you pray for me after the service? 'I guess we have to pray against cancer today. So let's do it now! Anybody who has cancer, come on up!"

He had changed the beginning of the service at Bethel Church to accommodate me, along with several others. God was at it again.

I walked up front along with six other people. Bill had us stand across the front, facing forward. For the next several minutes, Bill and a couple of his associates went down the line praying at length for each of us. As Bill put his thumbs in the palms of my hand I could feel heat radiating through them. Also I could feel the power of God as he prayed. His prayer was sincere, hopeful, and intense. I was moving in heavenly waters.

After the prayer time I floated back to my seat to listen to him preach.

He talked about how joy was our number one priority.

"The rest of life flows from joy. When we experience God's presence then we can feel comfortable in desiring other 'stuff 'like watching a movie. The reason is that God is in the ordinary and casual.

You can watch a movie as 'unto the Lord. 'Operate less from a sense of duty which drives out God's pleasure in our lives."

"Spiritual 'highs 'are not the 'best. 'All is the 'best. 'God is in it all. Wisdom is creativity with integrity. Don't control your walk with God. We do this 'good stuff 'for God, yet it feels empty. Why? It's 'religious. 'Instead let yourself feel God's presence with its pleasure and then get into life as it comes with its 'stuff. 'That is 'best.'"

The sermon articulated for me the trust that I already had in God's ability to heal. My efforts to find healing were "best." My living out my life of difficulties, comfort, and discomfort, was "best." God was with me here and now in the middle of my mess. Although I wanted it all to go away He was here until it did and beyond. He was my comfort in the storm while He was making the storm go away.

Bethel not only offered healing but also teaching which clearly laid out how supernatural healing worked. Afterwards I went up to get more prayer from the prayer team and received more encouraging messages before I left for home.

"God will show you 'secrets for healing 'as what to pray against and how to even 'smell 'what to pray for."

"Your daily style and spirituality is very controlled and all about 'being good 'so it is empty. Don't be afraid. Your prayer time is too obligatory and listening-based so you don't get into the day." (These words were like what I had heard in Stockton.)

"Against the spirit of hopelessness put on garments of praises; do not be discouraged or dismayed, have no spirit of condemnation. Peace - relax in God. Receive the promises of childhood again, dream again. Let go of regrets from past relationships. Stay in God's presence - Light casts out darkness." My tunnel was being lit again.

After this amazing trip, I journaled:

Jesus is described in the Gospel of John as the Light in the darkness. God was entering my inner cave where His Light did a better job of lighting the way than my little matchbooks.

I not only received prayer for healing at Bethel but also a new approach to finding it. I could praise God in the meantime. God could do anything, and even more importantly, God was wonderful. I could experience a level of joy while I waited. It was not only about getting healed. It was about getting more of God.

CHAPTER 23

More

After I had seen Rosie at the dance, when she encouraged me to visit Bethel Church, she called to tell me about a prayer service at Jubilee Christian Center in San Jose.

Despite my exhaustion, she admonished me to, "Keep fighting your spiritual battle despite the fatigue!" I agreed that I would attend yet another service.

I looked up the church online and drove for over an hour to the evening prayer service. Bathed in overhead lights, Jubilee sat by itself south of San Jose ringed by a huge parking lot.

I had arrived early for the formal service so I wandered around the church for a bit eventually finding my way into a small prayer group meeting. Since the meeting seemed to be informal I asked the leader, Bryan, for prayer. Suddenly he prophesied over me.

"There are more days in your book."

After the prayer meeting everyone adjourned to the main sanctuary where several hundred people gathered for the prayer service. The senior pastor opened the service and then invited Bryan to lead a prayer. He started by talking about me.

"We had a man come into our prayer group who asked for prayer against his cancer. Where is he? [I was leaning against a side wall because I did not feel well enough to sit down.] Oh, there he is. Everyone stand up and hold your hand up toward him. Pray with me for his healing!"

I stood there walloped by the impact of several hundred palms of hands aimed toward me. In this dreamlike moment I could hear

Bryan's prayers along with the murmured prayers of the crowd. The power of the Spirit literally swept over me. It went on for over a minute.

Then I leaned back against the wall relishing the moment as the service continued.

After the service a couple approached me and prayed for a clear brain and brain stem for me.

"You will do ministry again. God will elevate you. You will hear God. You will smell His Spirit. You will be blessed of Him." I took the alluding to "smelling" the Spirit as something like *tasting* the atmosphere created by God like the thick, warm humidity of a Caribbean rainstorm one cannot see but feels which feels much like the warm weightiness of a heavy cloak.

Within a few days Rosie invited me to another church where the Spirit was doing powerful things. Together we went to Blazing Fire Church in Pleasanton. That night the senior pastor, Brent, along with his wife prayed for my healing. Rosie and her friend saw a vision of flames coming off of me. Another woman envisioned red dots all over my body which seemed to identify my lymphoma diagnosis of cancerous lymph nodes throughout my body. A man named Art observed in his spirit a Pterodactyl (flying dinosaur) hovering above me.

Whenever I received such dramatic and unusual prayer I was always aware of God's loving and powerful presence. People would say all kinds of things to me. Some immediately would make sense to me and encourage me like the woman seeing my red dots. Others would say something that did not connect for me like the prediction for my healing that night or the Pterodactyl.

Typically in my spirit I could transmute these messages into something that made sense like I was being healed but just not completely. And so I always left strongly encouraged, rather than confused or skeptical.

The very next night I attended a church led by a married couple who were friends of mine. At New Hope Church in San Carlos Pastor Christie Pierce who was known for possessing a powerful gift of healing agreed to pray for me when the service ended. At that time, she walked over to tell her husband, Ben, to take care of the kids because she was planning to pray for me. In the ten seconds that it took for her to walk back to where I was sitting she heard God speak to her.

"It's in the bones."

She did not know that my lymphoma rested in my bone marrow, or "[I]n the bones."

She prophesied over me the words from Isaiah 55:2-3 which explained that I was in a covenant of love with God. He has rich food for you. So listen to God and eat what is good so you will delight in the richest of fare.

She continued, "You will have the bones of a five-year-old. A kernel of faith has opened in your heart. God will straighten your back and muscles. Be encouraged. His yoke is easy. I pray for peace in your head. Be free of pain. God has a new, special ministry for you. You will find it easier to communicate with God. God will trust you with things unlike most people. He stands about three feet away from you and watches. And He adores you."

Again my search for healing was leading to a new ministry call for me . . . once I was healed.

On the very next night I went again to Jubilee Christian Center for more prayer. I attended the pre-service prayer time where I received prayer from three pastors as well as the whole prayer group. I was told that this never happens. At the end of the prayer time yet another pastor prayed for me.

I discovered that with each of these formal prayer times the initial impact of the prayer was the most powerful. However as the power of the prayers seemed to lessen as more prayer flowed from the same person or church, the effect of the prayer stayed with me longer. It became cumulative and created a great momentum of hope in my spirit for healing.

Two months later Christie Pierce prayed over me again at New Hope Church, "Don't fear. You will receive huge joy. There is more. An eventual full healing is unknown. Today accept the words from Proverbs - 'Pleasant words bring healing for the bones.' You may feel you are in a sinking craft and crying out to God, 'Don't you care?' That's always our suspicion when it's very hard like now with chemo and nausea. But why do you fear? Where is your faith?"

During this time someone mentioned that a young faith healer who had dramatically exhibited the spiritual gift of healing was coming to the Bay Area. As usual I visited his conference. I arrived during the middle of one of his talks. I sat down and watched. He seemed to say whatever came into his mind while speaking with great energy and conviction.

Then he invited some folks to come forward for healing. A few people came up on stage and he prayed for them. I did not see much change after he prayed.

Suddenly he invited anyone with a terminal disease to come forward. Assuming that was why I was there I walked up to the front of the large auditorium along with four or five other people while hundreds watched us. Again within minutes of entering a service where I went for healing I became one of those identified and called forward as at Bethel and Jubilee.

We did not go up onto the stage but stood in front of it. He came down to us and walked down the line praying for us as Bill Johnson did at Bethel. I was first.

Unlike Bill who held my hands and prayed a very intense prayer this young man stood in front of me without touching me. He talked to me first.

"You have some kind of terminal disease?"

"Yes."

"What is it?"

"Cancer."

"What kind of cancer?"

"Non-Hodgkin lymphoma."

"OK."

He started praying forcefully while looking into my eyes. He lightly touched my shoulders and then blew gently into my face.

I felt surprised and dubious. It seemed to be almost offensive. I had never had someone blow in my face before and not for healing. I knew of laying on of hands to cause healing but never blowing in someone's face.

But then I got weak in my legs. I could still stand, but barely, and then I could not. It was not psychological and it was not the power of suggestion since he said nothing about my legs getting weak.

Eventually I went with it and sat down. Then I lay down. I felt great, like a baby wrapped in a blanket comfortably lying in his crib. I moved into a state of dozing while I lay on the floor. I did not care what anyone thought as I lay there in front of the stage. I was in a state of total peace. I vaguely noticed that the people to my right had done the same thing. I had no desire to get up. I do not know if anyone checked up on me or put a blanket on me.

Close to an hour passed. At least it felt like it. He long ago had gone back up on stage and kept teaching as if everything was normal. I did not feel stupid or embarrassed. It was wonderful. It was very restful and gentle.

Finally I woke up from my rest.

I tried to sit up. It felt like I was getting up in the morning on my day off, "Do I stay asleep and relax here in bed or get myself going?" That took about 10 minutes to decide. I finally resolved to get up. Then came the surprise.

I could not get up! As I attempted to rise I found that my legs would not work. My brain was telling my legs to walk but my legs were not getting the message. I had completely lost my sense of strength and balance. I was not dizzy but rather intoxicated.

Slowly I got to my knees and then lifted one leg . . . and then the other. I felt like when I was a little boy trying to ice skate for the first time. I could not do it. The closest seat was about 15 feet away. As I headed for it my legs veered me off in a 90 degree direction. I staggered badly while suddenly realizing that it was happening in front of all these people.

Then I veered the other way. Foot by foot I made my way to the seat. I plopped down. Slowly my head cleared. Finally I returned to normal.

These experiences did not heal me completely but they made my body feel well for a time. I think they helped my body to get used to what healing would feel like. Also they gave me enormous hope. This hope became integral to becoming healed. And I believe that physical healing had taken place albeit not completely. Step-by-step I was healing.

Occasionally I thought to myself, why do I have to drive to hear or meet a certain healer? I answered the question with the realization that millions of people had conversion experiences at Billy Graham Crusades because he had a unique and powerful gift of evangelism. When Billy Graham invited someone to come forward to meet Jesus that person felt compelled to come forward; he had this gift from God. I had experienced it myself at his crusades. The same phenomenon happened with these people who had a strong anointing from God to bring healing supernaturally. God moved through them with unusual power to heal.

CHAPTER 24

On the Road Again

On March 2, 2006, two years after her sudden decision to not do the transplant, Dr. Horning and I talked over the possibility of a transplant again.

I was back on the road to a transplant.

"In December of last year the lymphoma was in 80% of your bone marrow and 100% meant you would die. Today it is 70%. We can conclude that the chemotherapy has caused no improvement. Now the platelet numbers are better but we don't know why. Therefore the transplant is in order."

"Your prognosis of 11 or 12 years of life has now shrunk considerably. Your non-Hodgkin lymphoma was at stage four [the most dangerous stage] at the time of your diagnosis. Yet no diagnosis until stage four is common because it is so hard to discover; it stays below the radar because it is so slow moving."

"Get the transplant now while you are still relatively healthy. If you are so sick that I hospitalize you it's too late. So I must decrease the lymphoma to less than 50% of your bone marrow for you to tolerate the transplant. Since you have more than that and the chemotherapy did not remove it we will stop all treatment. We will let your body recover on its own over the next year. Then we will treat you again which will hopefully produce a better result."

The transplant would literally *transplant* some of my donor's bone marrow into me. The immune system has its home in the bone marrow. Since my immune system allowed cancer to enter my body it had failed to do its job. If I could find a compatible person whose immune system did not allow cancer and put some of their immune system into my body then perhaps my cancer would disappear. The donor's immune system would be transplanted in the form of their bone marrow going into my bone marrow where my immune system rested.

Dr. Horning wanted me to keep some of my bone marrow because it still protected me from other diseases like pneumonia and diabetes. If Stanford removed all my immune system during the transplant procedure I could die from even a bad cold.

Stanford intended to give me a drug called ATG to eliminate some of my bone marrow. The idea was to remove over half of my bone marrow. Then the transplanted bone marrow would become the majority, or over 50%, of my immune system and therefore have the efficacy to eliminate the cancer because it was the dominant immune system in my body.

A problem could arise by having the two immune systems co-exist in the same body. Any non-blending of the two immune systems was entitled *graft-versus-host disease* whereby the grafted or transplanted bone marrow would fight against rather than meld into the bone marrow of the host (my body). Half of all transplant patients acquired some amount of graft -versus-host disease; one third of those turned into serious autoimmune problems that lasted for the rest of the patient's life.

Then Dr. Horning told me of one more giant complication. "The transplant could lead to death! During the first year after the transplant, 20% of the patients die from infections or other complications," Dr. Horning solemnly explained. "But on the other side of the ledger it ends the cancer for 30% of the patients."

Since the more compatible the donor's bone marrow the better, a sibling donation would be best. I reached out to my brother and sister to get them tested to determine if either would be a compatible donor.

Dr. Horning then arranged my appointment with the oncologist who would shepherd me through the transplant process. I met Dr. Judith Shizuru on May 4. She immediately put me at ease with her very pleasant and easygoing nature. And like Dr. Horning she exuded confidence and competence. Moreover she was the person who had actually created this particular transplant that I would receive. Dr. Shizuru enthused that my cancer "exquisitely" fit this treatment.

A week later I returned to Dr. Horning.

"Now the clock is ticking so you need to get a match with your siblings or go to the national registry to find a match. Whichever donor you get it is a 'go. 'No point in waiting because now is when you're strong."

Another week later I learned that my brother was a perfect match - all 10 markers matched! Stanford used a system of 10 markers to quantify the qualification of a potential donor match with a patient. A perfect score of 10 was outstanding.

My medical treatment was all coming together. I was now receiving a transplant created by an oncologist at the top lymphoma center in the world under the care of one of the top lymphoma specialists in the world. And I had the perfect donor. This confluence of events gave me peace that this was the right course of action. I saw God's hand in this incredible combination of circumstances.

With these factors coming together so well and my continual dance with increasing and decreasing amounts of cancer in my bone marrow running me down emotionally I reached the point where I was ready to accept that a transplant was in order.

Then Dr. Horning passed me off to Dr. Shizuru, "She is excellent. Don't worry."

I called my brother with the news.

"I'll do it," he promised. He immediately stepped up to save my life when I needed his help the most. I guess it was payback for when he swiped my gumballs.

CHAPTER 25

Coverage

"I'm surprised that your insurance company denied the transplant," Stanford informed me.

I had focused so much on the risks surrounding the transplant I forgot that I had to pay for it. My health insurance plan provided by my ministerial denomination was great so the denial of coverage for the transplant astonished me. I regularly had been receiving my disability insurance with no trouble.

I had an unusual insurance plan. My denomination had been around for a long time so it had collected plenty of money. It could even self-fund its health insurance. In other words it did not have an insurance company pay for medical care for its ministers; instead it paid for their care from its own funds. And since it hired the pastors it covered, it had more compassion on its insured pastors than would a more impersonal insurance company, which led to a more generous attitude about providing coverage.

But now the compassion seemed to have ended.

Fortunately the insurance contact person at Stanford, Gary, offered wisdom, competence, humor and most importantly, perseverance.

Gary walked me along the painstaking path of appealing my denomination's decision. He informed me that the procedure was not cheap, "The treatment costs $200,000-$500,000 depending upon all the variables involved with this complicated procedure. The drugs and preparing the donor and patient is expensive. The infusion of the bone marrow into the patient alone costs $75,000-$100,000."

He also told me, "The problem lies in the fact that the insurance company's reviewing doctor considered the procedure to be *experimental* rather than *investigational.* Experimental means the procedure has not taken place often enough. Investigational means the procedure is beyond experimental."

It turned out that my denomination had an insurance company administer its health insurance, that is, while it did not have an insurance company pay the medical bills, it did use an insurance company to review medical claims to help the denomination determine which bills to pay. Thus the less compassionate more formalized procedure of an insurance company did come into play in my complicated medical case, after all. Therefore I somehow had to get past the normal insurance process to get to the more compassionate-minded denomination itself to approve payment for the transplant. This would be much harder than I realized.

I started my own investigation into the denial of my claim by calling the insurance company which processed my denomination's medical claims. I spoke with Tracy who thankfully would become my guardian angel. She knew about transplants and counseled me to never give up, "Keep appealing any denial of a claim."

Dr. Shizuru played her part by sending the insurance company a letter along with several charts to prove the appropriateness of the transplant.

Tracy called me back with the bad news, "Your appeal was denied because they still view it as experimental. Dr. Shizuru's documentation has not been published yet. You still have two more appeals, to another doctor inside of the insurance company and to a doctor outside of the insurance company."

Soon after, the "inside" doctor denied it. Shortly after that, Gary informed me, "Even though we flooded the 'outside 'doctor with Dr. Shizuru's published papers he denied your appeal. Dr. Shizuru even personally called him. He turned out to not specialize in transplants, had not read her papers, did not understand what she told him, and had already made up his mind."

Since I had exhausted the appeal process through the insurance company I went directly to the denomination. I spoke with Rhonda who was secretary to the appeals board for the denomination.

"We usually follow the insurance company's decisions but your case is unusual and more serious. I will continue to send it to more doctors. Those doctors can talk to Dr. Shizuru directly. If it still gets denied then it will end up with the denomination appeals board which is made up of the leaders of the financial arm of the denomination. They will review it from scratch. This board meets once a month and even sooner in cases of emergency. You can call me if you have questions."

So far this drama had lasted one month. As it unfolded I stayed calm. I lived my life now with the frame of mind that I figured this whole crazy deal of seeking healing was completely out of my hands and up to God, Who seemed still to be on the job. This latest conversation gave me some hope that the kind and good people of my denomination would figure out a way to work it out.

Dr. Shizuru's treatment plan was relatively new. The studies for her procedure only began five years earlier when a 10 year history was protocol for a procedure to receive general acceptance. In addition she wanted to only radiate one area where the cancer was most pronounced rather than the whole body as was the common practice. Also she wanted to give me ATG, an immunosuppressant, rather than another more commonly used drug which was more toxic. The old procedure had the goal of killing the cancer with drugs while her new treatment would use my brother's healthy transplanted bone marrow to kill the cancer.

When I saw Dr. Horning she suggested that I tell Gary, my insurance contact at Stanford, to, "Tell the next doctor in the line of appeal that the cost of the transplant is cheaper than the alternative treatments. The more commonly used drug, instead of the ATG that Dr. Shizuru wants to use, does not work. Dr. Shizuru's procedure is your only option because none of the chemotherapy-based treatments will work at this point to stop the cancer's growth. You have probably maxed out your ability to use any more chemotherapy anyway. This is your only chance - even the other older forms of bone marrow transplants will not work for you. And this newer approach is definitely not experimental."

When I spoke again with the secretary at the denomination she informed me she was not so sure that their office could find a bone marrow transplant specialist to review my case, somehow due to litigation concerns.

It appeared that my appeal attempts were stalling out.

But unbeknownst to me Tracy, from the insurance company, had been working overtime on my behalf. On one day she spent nine hours making sure that the ultimate decision-makers at the denomination got the true picture of my situation. When I spoke to her later she told me what happened.

"I believed that your case should definitely have been approved. And now it has!!"

Gary called and then Rhonda called with the same wonderful message, "I wanted to reach you with the good news."

The denomination would fully cover the heavy cost of the transplant!

CHAPTER 26

Dr. Miklos

Meanwhile my blood count was dropping. I was even receiving transfusions but they were not helping much. Dr. Shizuru wanted to get on with the transplant as I could not get much worse and still have the transplant.

But when cancer blocked 70% of my bone marrow again Dr. Shizuru had to postpone the transplant. She wanted me to return to Dr. Horning's care.

However Dr. Shizuru worked with a team of doctors whose collective decision outweighed hers. They wanted me to receive more chemo along with Rituximab, which I had never received together before. Dr. Horning had told Dr. Shizuru that she did not want to do that as she did not think it would work. Dr. Shizuru agreed with her. They all were to decide by the end of the week.

This large team of physicians met and decided that I should first undergo an experimental procedure before I could have my transplant. When Dr. Shizuru told me of the team's decision she was livid, visibly shaking. She believed in the transplant and wanted me to benefit from it as soon as possible. But they outvoted her.

I viewed this change in direction as I had responded to the insurance coverage ordeal. I *went along for the ride* believing as my mother had believed, "It all works out for the best." I had no control over any of it so what else could I do? I always felt His presence. I would survive the experimental treatment like I survived everything else.

But it still was unpleasant and worse, it did not work. A few weeks into the experimental treatment I wrote in my journal:

July 8, 2006 - Horrible night - could hear demons cry in one dream, and was talking with Satan in another dream about the success of some kind of oral presentation that I had just made. Satan appeared as an old, grizzled stockbroker, somewhat warm but with eyes full of deceit, dressed in a casual gold sweater and constantly wearing a full, duplicitous smile. I was drawn to explain it and convince him of the success of the day long conference presentation, knowing full well who he was. He was like Screwtape [from *Screwtape Letters* by C.S. Lewis], *waiting to eat me. I was like a moth to the candle.*

Rosie had called the previous night with prayer and encouragement. I had been heavy on her heart all week.

I wrote further, *I'm very uncomfortable with chemo. Can't sleep. Anxious . . .*

The dream meant to me I had some kind of spiritual battle going on within me. The spirit of darkness, with even demons perhaps, was harassing me. If God encouraged me then someone or something would counter that with deliberate discouragement. In the dream satan opposed my efforts to explain my impending success with scorn and derision behind a solicitous but duplicitous smile.

Apparently my dream uncovered the fact that deep within my subconscious I doubted more than I realized. My *go-along* attitude maybe did not cover all my misgivings. Perhaps my admitting any doubts to myself made me afraid which upset my inner balance. Perhaps.

Two days later I listened to a radio sermon by my friend Mark Labberton, Senior Pastor at First Presbyterian Church in Berkeley, now President of Fuller Theological Seminary. The sermon explained how God's Spirit made our lives holy right where we were. Gene called later in the day with the same message. Evidently even though I had misgivings, God was still working on my behalf providing a holy peace.

But then the next day brought more serious disappointment with news that Dr. Shizuru was departing on sabbatical for seven months. I would need a new transplant oncologist.

I looked to my oncological team for emotional, as well as medical, support because they were my medical mentors and experts. For one to leave felt like losing a parent. I lost my moorings for a moment. But

Dr. Horning comforted me, "The transplant is a bumpy ride. You'll like Dr. Shizuru's replacement. He is a researcher of immunology like Dr. Shizuru and a nice guy."

Soon after the tall and kindly Dr. David Miklos smiled his way into my patient room. In our first meeting he appeared a little nervous but conveyed authentic warmth and empathy. I could tell that he had to slow himself down to explain things to me, because his brain moved so much faster than his mouth. I liked that in a doctor.

Dr. Miklos walked me through the process of the transplant. It would take several months for my brother's bone marrow to grow enough to improve my immune system. However I should feel "good" through the recovery phase. I was to only let a few people see me during that time so as to avoid picking up some kind of infection. "Fewer people, less chance."

As he explained to me the statistics of success or failure with the transplant I realized that they did not really matter to me. I had to have the transplant according to my expert physicians. God had been with me until now. I only needed to win my race. The success and failure rates of anyone else did not matter. I had my own success and failure rate.

A week after that, Dr. Miklos said that the transplant was ready to go because the experimental treatment had not proven useful.

CHAPTER 27

The Warm-Up

"We always start on Sundays."

Suzanne, my new transplant nurse, gave me the layout and specifics.

I was to enter the hospital on a Sunday evening. Then early on Monday morning I would begin a five-day course of the ATG drug to decrease my volume of bone marrow. Also some radiation would begin on that first Monday.

Someone would pick me up at the hospital on Saturday, six days later, to go back to my nearby apartment in Menlo Park to rest. The following day, I would return to the Infusion Center in the Cancer Clinic for a check-up. On the Monday through Thursday of the second week, I would receive more radiation during the day and go home each evening. On that second Friday, I would receive my brother's donation of his bone marrow cells. (He would have received injections for several days to boost his immune system and undergone apheresis [harvesting of the cells from his blood].)

After I received my brother's donation on that second Friday, I would spend that night in the hospital for observation and go home on the following day. From then, I would have friends, my caregiver team, stay with me to watch over me and take me to the hospital for daily treatments and check-ups.

For me, these two first weeks would not feel very well. During the second week, especially, I would mainly have fatigue and food tasting issues.

It would take about 100 days in all to recover from the initial effects of the transplant. Around the midpoint of this recovery time, I might experience some fever or fatigue. Throughout the 100 days, I would make daily visits to the hospital which would taper off to every other day.

My caregivers, if possible, would have to attend a class to learn their multi-layered roles. Their main job would be to watch for any sudden change in my condition. I could get a fever within one hour. If I had a fever of over 100 degrees, I was to return to the hospital immediately.

Like a pre-game moment with the coach, I got to see Dr. Shizuru one more time before the transplant began. She made it a point to drop into the office while technically on her sabbatical. Her comments were encouraging and realistic.

"The time is ripe for you to have the transplant. This treatment is exquisite for your particular form of non-Hodgkin lymphoma. Now Don, it is not unreasonable to wait and re-check your bone marrow three months from now. Your cancer does not grow that fast. But it can transmute into a more aggressive type of non-Hodgkin lymphoma which would prevent your ever receiving the transplant. It will not go away on its own; I've never seen that. But the transplant can be fatal, ineffective, or eliminate the cancer."

I decided that now I was ready to get on with it. Two years previously, I had not wanted to suffer through it. Now I had changed.

With all the drama and angst that accompanied the cancer and the treatment, I lived in a constant state of an emotional and spiritual engagement. Impending death was always there. I made life-and-death decisions regularly. And as when accepting the chemo, I went with my *spiritual gut*. I trusted God was influencing my decisions and desires. The timing felt right now to go ahead with it. I was ready.

CHAPTER 28

Game On

Then came that fateful Sunday afternoon in 2006 when I quietly slipped into Stanford Hospital with my suitcase and briefcase. Led to my empty, sterile room I changed into a hospital gown and climbed into the clean bed.

As I sat up in bed with my anxiousness my friend Linda dropped by with a well-crafted tuna cocktail and good wishes. I thought it was a nice idea until my stomach reconsidered.

Then it was as if the Cal band marched into my room when my long-time friend Kent stormed in with a huge smile on his face. Kent had been born under a sun that said ENTHUSIASM! Kent had not only been a member of the marching band during his years at Cal but was also a cheerleader during those Viet Nam War years when non-cheering cynicism was popular.

We had backpacked through Yosemite in a rainstorm dodging lightning bolts and relaxed in the solitude of a pristine mountain lake. He was the guy who had soloed a cappella at my father's memorial service, *What a Wonderful World.*

Next my good friend Gail called me to ask about my condition. We talked for half an hour. Gail helped me immeasurably gathering items for my home like special sheets and towels. Now she had volunteered to send emails to my friends about my condition as the transplant recovery progressed. She wrote to everyone that I, "Sounded great on the phone."

Then it began. I received my first dose of ATG and nodded off to sleep. In the wee hours, many strident voices in my room rudely awakened me. Evidently my temperature had spiked, so after much muttering I found my bed (with me in it) rolling on a circuitous ride to the darkened intensive care unit in the center of the hospital. I had not even been in the hospital for one night before the team's well-planned schedule went askew.

After arriving in the ICU I fell back to sleep and slept and slept. I sometimes would notice some movements and shadows to my right from a clinician sitting in front of monitors and watching me. Apparently I had my own personal ICU nurse.

The curtains around my room had designs that seemed to morph into cars, and then stones, and then animals, which danced across the fabric.

Occasionally people would poke their heads between the curtains, look at me, and disappear.

Finally I awoke from my sleep to a brightly lit ICU room and the concerned face of Dr. Miklos staring at me.

As I slowly regained fuller consciousness I tuned into what he was saying, ". . . We can stop the whole thing right now and go back to the way things were. Or we can move ahead."

Before thinking it over I impulsively responded, "Let's keep going. There's no alternative," which was true.

With a slight smile on his face Dr. Miklos just said, "Okay," and turned and left the room. Later that morning I returned to my patient room.

Months later Dr. Miklos and I discussed that trip to ICU.

"You had a temperature of 104 degrees!"

"Wow, that night I was in ICU . . . "

"Four nights . . ."

I had no idea.

Back in my patient room, I found a note that my friends Terry, a pastor in training, and Hudd, the retired physician on the healing team at church, had left for me after one of their two visits to see me in ICU.

,DonTerry B and I were just passing by and knew you were having a tuff time, but TONS of prayers are going up and we all count on Jesus 'loving care, will and ability - we all want total cure! You are in our dreams and minds, Love, Hudd and Terry.

Meanwhile Gail wrote to everyone about my trip to ICU and asked for prayer.

So many people prayed so many prayers for me during my cancer. I know that they saved me. I will always be grateful.

Every time I read Hudd's and Terry's note I get tears in my eyes as I realize how alone I was. Yet in my aloneness I always felt a presence of God along with the love of my family and friends.

Now that I survived ICU I had to continue to take the ATG to prepare for the transplant. The more of it I took, the more that my bone marrow evaporated which had the nasty side effect of making me exceptionally and uncontrollably rude.

I could not control my irascibility. I ordered nurses around no matter how nicely they treated me. I had them move my belongings around just for the heck of it. My body, and evidently my mind, rebelled against this drug making me into a tyrant.

Finally Dr. Miklos came in one evening to lecture me on being civil to the staff. All I felt was that he was not sharing my experience of lying in that bed with this stuff in him. He had no idea. He left and I kept fuming.

When I completed the nasty administration of the ATG my rudeness ended. To the great relief of everyone I left the hospital for home.

Meanwhile my brother, the avid cyclist, found peace by riding his bike every day. When I arrived home he regaled me with stories about riding in the hills and on busy roads navigating his way between semi-trucks and commuter traffic. He had faithfully received his Neupogen shots to boost his white blood count which in fact had caused him significant bone pain despite the medical team's promise to the contrary.

Finally the day came for the actual transplant. I went to the hospital and sat in a soft chair. The nurse who had harvested my brother's bone marrow the day before brought it to me in a large plastic bag, like a normal pint of blood. She gave it to me as an intravenous infusion. As simple as that. The transplant over.

The preparation leading up to the transplant and the recovery from the transplant took a long time and caused most of the problems. The actual transplant took my brother a few hours and took me about an hour. It was the easiest part of the entire procedure.

The completion of the actual transplant came about so quickly and suddenly after all that discomfort that it almost passed by unnoticed.

Without fanfare I went home to my apartment and my brother gratefully departed for his home. My brother had *ridden to the rescue* by enduring his own painful challenges to enable the donation. He had incarnated Lance Armstrong to me in my race against death.

CHAPTER 29

Caregiving

As part of my planning I had put out the word that I needed *a few good men* to live with me for a week at a time, to watch over me, prepare my meals, wash my clothes and bedding, *keep house*, and *hang out*. And incredibly they came.

Friends used up week-long vacation time from work. Some jumped on airplanes to fly over several states to be with me. Wives allowed their husbands to take off for a week. I was humbled and amazed.

Other friends from my church and community became "captains" who supervised the caregivers. The captains had to take the transplant patient care courses at Stanford Cancer Clinic to train and supervise the caregivers who could not take the courses since they did not live nearby.

My venture capitalist company Chief Financial Officer friend handled all the Advance Directive, will, and mortuary documentation.

"I'll pull the plug on you, Don," he told me with a smile. If the worst happened and I lapsed into a coma, the hospital staff would need someone to allow them to ignore the requirement to provide extraordinary measures, like putting me on a breathing machine. He was that person because I had given him Power of Attorney over my personal matters.

These caregiver friends came without expectations. I do not recall any who said, "No."

I had taken the precaution of re-writing the lengthy binder provided by the Cancer Clinic that outlined all the care and precaution requirements for transplant patients, into my own "Caregiving Manual," shaved down to a mere 64 pages!

It was full of highlighted sentences, bold print, and italicized duties.

"If you are ill, or have been exposed to someone ill and feel that you may be carrying any illness, please let [names of my supervising captains] and me know ASAP before you come so they can make other arrangements!" Comments like these *welcomed* my caregivers to my home.

The introduction said, "My immune system will be greatly depleted, and my condition can *go south* quickly!"

One caregiver later told me of his fear during his week with me of possibly passing along some unknown flu or virus. Another said that he did not want me to get sick on his *watch*.

I entitled a portion of my manual with the warm, fuzzy, "YOU". It even described their appropriate attitude, "Among your tasks will be maintaining a positive attitude, calm demeanor and flexible approach . . . humor is a good thing."

And if visitors dropped by: "When they arrive: the Caregiver is to greet all guests at the door. Don cannot stand before an open door without his mask!!! Have them enter and instruct them to stand just inside the door and remain there. Then close the door! The door needs to be closed at all times and not kept open more than absolutely necessary. Then go tell Don he has a guest. Don will take it from there."

Apparently my manual subconsciously served as a personal journal where I expressed my deepest anxiety without knowing it. Again perhaps my laissez-faire attitude about my cancer may have only semi-successfully covered my powerful misgivings about my illness.

My caregiver's daily routine called for them to prepare breakfast, drop me off at the nearby cancer clinic for daily follow-up care, return home to clean the apartment from all dust and bacteria, *savor* their allotted four hours of personal time, pick me up from the hospital, perhaps take me for a short walk, hang out with me, prepare dinner for us, and then watch a movie. To make it as entertaining as possible I had obtained a large DVD library and set up an account with the then-new Netflix for our *viewing pleasure*. And we watched A LOT of movies, often back to back (when we were not watching sports).

When I was at home the caregivers had to check on me often to be sure that my condition had not suddenly plummeted. If it exceeded 100.4 twice in two hours or was over 101.3, we had to call the cancer clinic immediately, or if at night, rush to the hospital. The concern was that an infection could develop quickly because of my depressed immune system. There was always the risk that I could go into septic shock which could be fatal.

I was vulnerable to all kinds of infections: bacterial, fungal, and viral. The caregivers had to wash their hands with antibacterial soap frequently and dry them with paper towels - lest the cloth towels collect bacteria. Also they had to place alcohol-based hand cleaners around the apartment. They had to dust and vacuum so that bacteria would not settle on my furniture. To keep the dust down we had to keep all doors and windows closed. They had to go to the extent of wiping the doorknobs with a cleaning agent. They even had to wear *indoor shoes*.

When I travelled to the cancer clinic every day I had to take along my backpack, which included my protective mask (the HEPA filter mask that made me look like a fly) and my medications. Also, I brought my paperwork: a daily chart listing all of the symptoms noticed by my caregivers, a chart listing my caloric and fluid intake as filled out by my caregivers, a list of new questions, the manual provided by the cancer clinic, and a calendar of my appointments. Further, I had to bring along my essentials: reading glasses, watch, extra clothing (in case I was admitted to the hospital), reading materials, portable DVD player and DVD, hat, small Bible, journal, ear plugs, cell phone and charger, address and phone lists, water bottles with cold boiled water, food, electric razor, mouthguard, and cane. Fortunately I did not have to carry the pack.

For reference I provided the caregivers with a list of 18 different medical professionals for any medical problem which might arise!

The cancer clinic manual provided a full list of symptoms for caregivers to watch for: shortness of breath, dry cough, low fever, blood in the urine, difficulty swallowing, persistent nausea, vomiting, diarrhea, runny nose, congestion, body aches, unusual headaches, blurred vision, and bleeding.

Also the caregivers also had to cook, or at least try. There were many food restrictions, such as no raw foods, fast foods, food with gluten, or food kept in the refrigerator for over 24 hours. The cooking instructions went on for eight pages.

They had to boil and cool the drinking water; I could not even drink store bought bottled water. I had to drink at least three quarts of water per day.

I could go outside for walks if I wore the HEPA mask. The transplant would make me very sensitive to the sun so I had to wear protective clothing.

As for laundry the caregivers had to wash sheets and towels, along with dirty clothes, every three days. I set up a code system so they always used the correct temperature. Also the laundry duties included lugging the bags of clothing and linens to and from the community laundry facility on the far side of the complex. One caregiver even took the time to re-write the laundry directions into a Tip Sheet.

And then there were the checklists. The caregivers had to check the boxes on a detailed To-Do list - every day. "Did you take off your outside shoes and put on your inside shoes every time you entered the apartment? Did you maintain the Yellow Spiral Notebook with your observations on Don's ongoing condition? Did you remind Don two or three times per day to take his temperature? Did you clean the kitchen dishes, countertops, and dining table? Did you replace the kitchen sponges?"

CHAPTER 30

My Guests

If married I could have had a wife help take care of me. But I am glad that I did not have to burden someone whom I loved with my long-term battle with cancer. It was tough enough carrying the emotional load of a terminal diagnosis. To watch the sadness settle into the heart of a wife would have made it much harder.

I felt alone sometimes but not that often. I had adjusted to my situation relatively well, under the circumstances. And without being inauthentic, I felt an abiding peace that filled the emotional gap of living without a partner.

And I really was not alone. Here is where my relationship with God came to the fore. I did not simply acknowledge some belief in God's company; I tangibly felt it all the time. I never felt deeply alone. Someone truly was there, inside of me, with a warm love.

But my physical aloneness evaporated when my caregivers arrived.

Each *guest* or caregiver appeared with his suitcase in hand and carrying a lot of uncertainty and compassion. I would open the front door for each new arrival to find each one standing there with a perplexed and concerned look on his face. None of them knew what to expect beyond what I had provided in the manual. One of them told me later that the comprehensive manual that I had prepared was unambiguous as to "What" needed to be done and "When," but was unclear as to "How" to do the various required tasks.

Usually when I first met them at the door they were surprised that I looked so good. To them I looked almost normal. They found that they could settle in more easily than they had feared. Though I needed them to provide some specific care and chauffeur me to the hospital daily, more than anything, I needed their company. As a people-person I always loved company. For me it was an ongoing reunion with old friends. Every time I opened the door I was excited. It was almost fun.

After the first caregiver's arrival, the caregiver who was leaving would stick around to update his replacement about my status. For instance, for a period of time I had a constant stare on my face. Recovering from the transplant was like living out the movie, *Invasion of the Body Snatchers*. The outgoing caregiver had to warn the next guy to not freak out when he saw me always staring at him. Eventually the stare faded.

When I remembered I would take the two caregivers 'picture at the *changing of the guard*.

The assigned captain would usually drop by to help the new caregiver become acclimated to the apartment's environment and familiar with performing his expected duties.

My first caregiver, Terry, who had flown in from out of state, had it easy since I was stuck in the hospital with an infection for the entire week. He spent the time with his daughter and friends who lived nearby. During that week my cardiologist friend Dave visited me in the hospital and noticed my pronounced mental confusion. He drove home in tears believing that I had reached the end. Fortunately he was wrong.

My next caregiver, Jeff, is a benevolent, understanding soul who I met in seminary. After staying in the hospital for a week and a half I called him to ask him to pick me up on the day before Thanksgiving. Since he was single and very generous with his time I hoped that he could care for me over the holiday which he graciously did.

I called him in the morning having just been told that I would be released that afternoon. I told him to find the doors in the hospital with the big red X's on them, that admonished, Do Not Enter. I instructed him to go through the imposing doors anyway which he found to be an incredibly surreal experience.

After successfully navigating ourselves out of the huge hospital he drove me home. We decided that despite our being bereft of Thanksgiving fare we could not risk his exposure to a grocery store teeming with last minute shoppers. Instead I asked him to call one of my captains to ask for a last minute Thanksgiving shopping *spree* to collect whatever grub he or she could find.

A little while later the doorbell rang and there stood Allan, as Jeff described it, a retired CEO of a nearby corporation with a gentle smile holding two bags of "Safeway's best." The next day offered beautiful weather as we enjoyed our repast. I finally felt good in body and soul.

Jeff got me settled into my apartment after the *adventures* in the hospital. Conscientious, he organized all the details as to the innumerable tasks for everyone to do. He started the laundry, chauffeuring, and cooking routines. His thoroughness gave me peace in a very turbulent moment.

However by the time my third caregiver arrived my body started to rebel again. One day it took an hour for Will, along with David, another one of my captains, to lift me gingerly out of my bed to get me dressed and into a wheelchair to take me to the hospital. I was dead weight. Along with the breakdown of my strength came a return of my irascibility. I was rude and authoritarian, constantly giving orders even for minor things. But he hung in there with good-natured patience for the entire week until he gratefully passed me off to the next *unsuspecting soul*.

Thankfully I started to perk up as the Christmas season approached with its topsy turvy schedules making it challenging for anyone to find spare some time to stay with me. The pastor intern at Menlo Park Presbyterian, Terry, who had visited me in ICU with Hudd, stayed with me three different times to fill in the open slots in my schedule. His wife Patti was very gracious in allowing Terry to get away. Terry's relaxed, low-key manner eased me through the confusing holiday, transplant recovery days and nights.

Also Mark, a member of the Menlo Park Presbyterian cancer support group, stayed with me long enough to convince me that Aaron Neville could rhapsodize some entrancing New Orleans style Christmas carols.

Jeff came back for a second *tour of duty* by the time Christmas arrived. Some friends had kindly decorated my home and Gail catered a wonderful Christmas meal for us. Jeff had volunteered to stay through Christmas knowing that my other caregivers would be with their families.

I had returned to a reasonable level of comfort by the time my next caregiver and close friend from high school, Cliff, and I took some walks around the neighborhood. He recalled later, "Venturing outdoors for an attempt at reintroducing exercise to your routine, we looked like Sir Edmund Hillary and Tenzing Norgay (his assisting sherpa) and proceeded at about the same pace as those two mountaineers as they culminated their Mount Everest ascent. You, emulating Sir Edmund, were outfitted in a ski cap and parka. A twin filter rubber mask covered your nose and mouth. You gripped a walking stick in your gloved hand. I shuffled alongside, keeping a vigilant watch on my taller comrade. The entire expedition did not cover more than a short neighborhood block, but for someone recovering from the physical trauma of a bone marrow transplant and operating without the benefit of a functioning immune system, the effort was not unlike navigating the final few steps leading to the very top of the world."

He quickly discovered a significant difference between our schedules. I rarely emerged from my bedroom before 11 in the morning and therefore did not head toward bed until midnight. Later one of my caregivers, Kim, feared that my sleeping so late meant that something horrible had happened but just as he was about to peek into my room, he would hear me rustling around. Once Jeff had entered the bedroom to wake me for a trip to the hospital to get more Potassium, "I was standing there," he said, "and you were pale and I couldn't see any signs of breathing. I stood there for what seemed like minutes and thought you were dead. I shook you and then you breathed."

A typical day involved my *Awakening* where I glacially returned to consciousness and then moved my body one limb at a time to lift myself from repose, hence the rustling sounds that my caregivers would hear from outside my bedroom door. After washing my face I would enter the living room to greet my caregiver and then proceed if I could to prepare a mound of gluten-free hot cereal for breakfast.

Next I would ride along with my caregiver to the clinic for yet another examination and infusion. After passing the afternoon there my caregiver would bring me home where he or I would make dinner.

Instead of withdrawing into their worlds of small screens of cell phones or iPads my caregivers always joined me in watching shows. We enjoyed the British comedy *Bertie and Wooster* about a twenty-something man whose aunt paid for a butler to take care of him which was not too far from the reality of my situation. Otherwise we enjoyed my DVD collection watching one movie after another.

Another caregiver, a high school close friend named Dave, had brought *Man on the Moon* which he assumed was a comedy because it followed the life of *Saturday Night Live 's* Andy Kaufman. However it turned out to portray his unsuccessful battle with cancer so we stopped that one in a hurry. (It did not really bother me as I had adjusted to having cancer by now but I did not want to watch a sad movie about it.) Otherwise we watched as many professional football and college basketball games as possible thanks to the National Football League playoffs taking place then.

Another caregiver, Steve, and I watched Ken Burns's baseball documentary and reminisced about our beloved San Francisco Giants having grown up during the era of Willie Mays, Juan Marichal, and Willie McCovey.

As the weeks moved along caregivers annotated my manual that I left in my home. One said that it served as an, "Idiot proof guide with caregiving by the numbers." But as my radiologist friend and caregiver Paul learned the *hard way*, the manual demanded that they always take off their *outdoor shoes* and immediately wash their hands after taking out the garbage, or they would hear about it from me.

I surprised these men that I did not get more angry with God. Except for that terrible week early on with Will they noticed that I surrendered to God with a patient faithfulness. They told me I seemed sure of the outcome thus was unafraid of dying. One of them said that my example changed his prayer life.

My last caregiver, Bill, was the leader of our men's group. He commented how much he enjoyed the conversations as did one of the other members of our men's group, Ron, who filled in for a few days. We found deep fellowship in those dinner conversations.

CHAPTER 31

Transition

"Your 100 days are over. The caregivers may go home."

Dr. Miklos gave me the good news after only 90 days had passed.

He exclaimed that, "I have never seen a bone marrow biopsy show absolutely no cancer in the bone marrow on only Day 90 after a transplant! I've been telling the other oncologists about it!"

Again the incredible was happening.

"Your PET/CT result does still show some lymph nodes with cancer but don't panic. I'm not. The cancer isn't in your bone marrow which is the most important area. Your brother's bone marrow has 90% grafted with your body which is very good! The graft is almost complete. Very unlikely that it will relapse."

I had moved into Phase Two of the post-transplant schedule.

This excellent news began the year of 2007. My first journal entries reflected my upbeat frame of mind:

This will be a restoration year with an unknown, but good, future.

Goal for this year - listen better to God and others. Slow down.

Ecclesiastes says - Future - find joy in toilsome work, live divine life simply. Eat and drink with gladness. It's not about power. It's humility and accepting His provision with gratitude.

With these lofty goals in mind I moved into the next phase of my recovery.

Some restrictions ended. I no longer had to boil a large pot full of water, put it in the freezer to cool, and then transfer it to the refrigerator to keep cool, in order to get a drink.

But I still could not get a haircut at a shop or go to church. My bone marrow had not yet returned and as Dr. Miklos said to me, "The soil has been sown with new bone marrow seed which will take time to grow. That will take a year."

A few months later my bone marrow biopsy and PET/CT test results were perfect; the graft match looked, "Great," according to Dr. Miklos. Very importantly I suffered from NO graft versus host disease! Dr. Miklos enthused that I was doing, "Fantastic," and the transplant was a, "Huge success!"

With my many appointments with Dr. Miklos our relationship grew closer. We talked about his family and background as well as my thoughts and dreams about the future. I had not been dreaming about the future for a very long time.

At the next men's group meeting, Bill, asked me, "What do you want to do now?" Frankly I did not know.

In my prayer time the next day I heard in my spirit, "You give them something to eat!" Jesus had given his disciples the same illogical command when He ordered them to feed over 5,000 people who had been with them for a long time.

Then I heard what Jesus had told Peter, "Feed My sheep!" He had given Peter this command three times as described in John 21, after Peter had denied Him three times on the night before Jesus' Crucifixion.

So together these two commands meant to me that I was to resume my ministry profession in some manner.

As the months progressed, I gained an awareness of the *new me* back in the real world outside of my home. I was older and changed. My cardiologist Dave told me I was losing the narcissism that I had needed to survive the cancer.

In my journal I wrote that I was now, *.More amped and cramped* I wanted to get back into life. On the anniversary of my transplant I wrote in my journal, *!I feel like I am back* To celebrate the moment I slept 15 hours!

CHAPTER 32

Lenny

Phase Two was more open-ended than Phase One. The tightly scheduled, caregiver-driven weeks after my transplant gave way to a more normalcy. The cancer had largely left my body although pockets of it still showed up on tests. I was not ready to return to work due to lack of energy.

I spent 2008 recovering.

I continued to visit the physicians and staff at the Cancer Clinic regularly and get tested to look for any recurrence of the cancer. One highlight of this in-between time was interacting with Lenny.

He always entered the room with a concerned and haggard look yet always too with a warm and authentic smile. Lenny was the medical assistant who regularly visited cancer patients in the large infusion center. While we were sitting there usually too tired to watch our TV screens he would drop by to converse with us.

Lenny was the considerate person who allowed me to process my emotional turmoil by asking him questions and then more questions. Lenny had the dual gifts of compassion and patience both in vast measure. He would listen always . . . in smiling silence. I would vent, or question, or theorize. With as few words as needed and an ability to repeat himself again and again politely when necessary, he would respond to every question or comment. His insights invariably allayed my concerns.

I always came prepared for his visits. I brought a yellow pad with my questions which usually filled an entire page. Sometimes they were the same questions as the last time. It did not matter. He would answer all of them.

I had a sore chest, itchy mouth, indigestion, dizziness, food issues, catheter problems, dressing troubles, test result confusion, respiratory struggles, headaches, platelet decline, cleanliness worries, mask complications, potassium decline, fever, eye maladies, sore mouth, night sweats, reflux, pulse increase, anemia, and more. Lenny would calmly say, "Tell me everything."

What a gift to have someone listen to *everything*! He never ended one of our conversations without answering every one of my questions; he even gave me his direct number to call in an emergency.

Lenny was one reason I made it. I needed a confidant for my medical issues, someone *on the inside* who was on my side. The physicians were wonderful - very warm and engaging as well as knowledgeable and thorough. But their time was more limited than Lenny's. Along with them I needed someone who could de-brief my physician appointments - temporize them, make them more palatable, help me deal with them in more bite-size portions. That person was Lenny.

He offered me the truth wrapped in a glove of comfortable wisdom. I always felt better after my treatment sessions despite having some weird drug pumped into my body as we talked. Lenny made me feel safe.

CHAPTER 33

The Lesion

After all my unusual health issues I thought going to the ear doctor to check out some hearing loss would be no big deal. But he had me go through yet another MRI to check for a tumor next to my ear which was a regular practice for all his patients. Although the MRI did not find a tumor by my ear it found one in my brain.

It flabbergasted me! Dr. Miklos had given me glowing reports. I felt good. Everything seemed fine. Like my initial diagnosis it blindsided me.

It was 2009.

Dr. Miklos, Dr. Recht (my oncology neurologist), and the oncology radiologist quickly conferred. A spinal tap was done. Another MRI was performed. A biopsy was performed on the lesion (tumor). After a PET/CT exam they discovered the lymphoma in other places as well. They found that the cancer had returned.

In short the transplant had failed!

The doctors concluded that I should receive some very aggressive chemotherapy. They now considered extreme options.

The sudden bad news shocked me but did not entirely surprise me. Since my original diagnosis I had always lived with a certain sense of *borrowed time*. As the fellow support group member had said to me, "Nobody knows what it is like until the doctor tells YOU that you have cancer!" Cancer made my life uncertain. While my faith gave me an ongoing peace it did not eliminate all apprehension. They co-existed in an quiet tension.

When Dr. Miklos entered my patient room for our first appointment after the discovery of the lesion he did not walk in with the typical bounce in his step or talk with his usual sense of purpose. He seemed to have lost his enthusiasm. He even projected a level of hopelessness. He more or less muttered about my options.

Then all a sudden he stopped himself and took a long look into my eyes.

"This doesn't scare you, does it?"

My apparent calm surprised him. He said that normally his patients are much more anxious about death than I appeared to be.

I became self-conscious. I had not thought about it. I had always kept on going. He looked at me mystified while I shrugged my shoulders back at him. He smiled and mumbled something like, "Amazing," and then kept telling me about my options. I think my attitude lifted his hopes.

Meanwhile Dr. Horning did not share the depth of concern of the other doctors. She was not sure that the cancer was spreading; not sure where the cancer was coming from; not sure if the PET/CT showed that the cancer had returned; and not sure if the bone marrow transplant had knocked out all the non-Hodgkin lymphoma in the first place. At the very least this newly-discovered cancer was not aggressive or moving quickly. But she said that my case was indeed unique.

The next day I saw Dr. Horning again. She surprised me with the terrible news that she was leaving to go to an excellent research position at Genentech! My care was to move to one of her colleagues. As with Dr. Shizuru leaving I felt abandoned. But that had worked out well with my move to Dr. Miklos. My other physicians were excellent. There was always hope . . . and yet she was a world expert!

After all these doctors discussed my situation thoroughly they decided upon my receiving a small "boost" of my brother's bone marrow administered in a much abbreviated fashion. As Dr. Miklos told me later Dr. Horning had blithely suggested to him, "Why don't you just throw more of his brother's bone marrow at him and see what happens?" As in the football games of my youth my future now came down to the medical equivalent of a *Hail Mary* pass play on the last play of the game, which implied an unlikely probability of success.

I called my brother who did not understand how someone who appeared so healthy with a strong heart would break down so easily.

He wondered if the cancer had ever ended at all. But he generously agreed to go through the abbreviated process to provide me more of his bone marrow.

On my father's birthday in 2009 I received the second infusion of my brother's bone marrow. Since the procedure was greatly simplified, neither he nor I had to go through the level of preparation that we had in 2006. We simply sat in our chairs and donated, or received, blood with bone marrow in it.

Thankfully my denomination covered the cost again.

CHAPTER 34

Resurrection

Around the time of the bone marrow boost from my brother I attended a tiny healing conference at a nearby church. It was a low-key affair. I received some prayer, listened to a message, and felt more encouraged.

At the meeting someone mentioned that a few people were meeting on the next Tuesday evening to watch a DVD about a woman who actually had prayed her two-year-old son back from the dead. I figured, why not?

I arrived at the lonely and virtually empty church on that dark Tuesday night. I did not know where the DVD viewing would take place. I had to search out someone who could help me which turned into several people sending me in opposite directions. Finally someone said to try the children's education room somewhere on the second floor.

I climbed yet another flight of stairs to find the room right in front of me. The room held small children sized tables and chairs strewn around the floor. I joined four other people as one of them prepared the DVD for us and sat down in one of the small chairs.

As we peered at the DVD on a small screen in the corner it surprised me to see that the woman was not speaking from a big, well-lit stage at some large conference but at a normal church service. She told her story as if she were reporting on her vacation trip, with little fanfare.

It turned out that when her husband and she had gone out to dinner one evening they had left their two-year-old boy in the care of her husband's parents on their farm. Later in the evening the boy wandered out of the house and fell into a pond where he drowned.

The grandparents sadly called them from the hospital where they had taken him. The mother and her husband raced to the hospital to find their little boy in the emergency room on a life-support machine where he was no longer breathing on his own.

When she entered her son's room she immediately pronounced aloud, "Satan I know you came to kill, steal, and destroy, but you will not take my son! Jesus, You can do all things so heal my son! And so my son in the name of Jesus Christ wake up!" At that moment his vital signs re-started!

He had miraculously returned to life. However over the following days he did not improve. Undaunted she moved into his hospital room and never left. She prayed for him and sang over him incessantly. She would not let any non-medical personnel, like a well-wisher, family member, or friend, into the room unless they believed that he would fully recover.

After five days the doctors met with the parents to inform them that their son was brain dead. They showed them the films which displayed dark portions of his brain where life did not exist. They said it was time to give up. But the mother refused. The doctors were not pleased.

Her vigil continued until the ninth day when her son woke up! He could now function on his own but he still had no mental faculties. Her friends tried to console her with the news that at least her son was alive. But she was having none of it. She wanted him fully recovered so she continued her vigil.

Over time he slowly got better. Then finally after one full month from the date of his drowning he returned to normal. He walked out of the hospital completely recovered. It was a true miracle.

After the DVD ended the presenter in our little classroom said that the mother was now living in the San Francisco Bay Area and that she would lead a class about healing for several weeks. In fact the class was open to the public at a church only an hour from where I lived. On top of that the first class would start next week.

Benny Hinn had come to Oakland near where I lived. The young faith healer had come to Fremont near where I lived. Bill Johnson's church sat only four hours away. Jordan Seng had come to Palo Alto near where I lived. Christie Pierce lived near where I lived. And now this mother was coming to where I lived. The hope of heaven kept coming to me!

Her timely arrival into my world slowed the rising frustration from my horrible news about the lesion. I never reached a place of anger because of the failed transplant since her story was so compelling and hopeful. I felt that I still had a chance.

I showed up, writing pad in hand, to her first class. The accommodations surprised me again. Instead of a room we met in the large foyer of the church where it sold the food and coffee on Sunday mornings. Many chairs, couches, and small tables sat scattered haphazardly around the wide-open space which made it more difficult to focus on the speaker. The room felt cool and drafty with a slight odor of coffee wafting about.

Further I had assumed that hundreds of people would attend to hear this miraculous healer but the crowd only totaled a couple of dozen. Taking place on a weekday morning did make it unavailable to more who had to work.

Nonetheless I came ready to take it all in.

When the meeting started she walked up front to the middle of the foyer and immediately made it her own. An attractive woman in her mid-30's she emanated an even richer inner beauty. As she spoke with a constant expectant smile on her face God's righteousness poured from her as it had from Rita Bennett. She stood there exuding the vapor of God's Spirit. Her words were not so much heard as experienced. This woman knew God.

The effect of her presence caused hope to arise in the room. Unafraid she swept us into her world as she told us of her son's healing and how that healing power could work in all of us. My hope for my healing moved closer to certainty as I immersed myself in her encouraging words. I moved toward fully believing that my healing would happen.

During her teaching time I could hear and see little kids running around behind us. She pointed out her son who now was six years old. He seemed normal with no evidence of his drowning experience.

After the class I introduced myself to her mainly because I wanted to look her in the eyes and have her tell ME about her son's miraculous healing. As she shared the story with me I saw total authenticity gazing back at me. Apparently it really happened. Again I saw and heard for myself an amazing, inexplicable work of God.

Over the following weeks I had a private prayer time with her along with her husband. And I met her son who was a strong, healthy boy.

During that time, she taught us about the essence of her faith, that she viewed the Bible as not only true but having power within itself. By our praying relevant verses about healing over and over, the Spirit of God would release because it was God's Word that was being spoken. Since His Spirit moved through people to write the Bible, His Spirit resided in the words that were written in the Bible. When certain Scriptures were repeated by us aloud, His Spirit which lived in those words would sink down into our spirits and release power. I had never heard of that before.

She mentioned the writings of Charles Capps who wrote that healing could come from repeatedly saying aloud healing Scriptures like I Peter 2:24 that by Jesus' wounds we are healed!

CHAPTER 35

Hope Meets Faith

I came to understand this teaching in this way.

Jesus often told those who received healing from Him, "Your faith has healed you." What did that mean? I thought Jesus healed them, not their own faith. The answer appeared to lay in one verse. Hebrews 11:1 states that faith is being sure of what we hope for.

Apparently faith begins with hope. Now when you want something you automatically begin to hope for it. When we were young we wanted to go to Disneyland. Occasionally our parents would mention that someday we would go to this paradisal spot which made us hope that we would go there. With each comment or hint by them our hope grew. But it was not until they parked our car in the parking lot and we started walking toward those gates that we were sure that we definitely were going to Disneyland. Then we believed. Then we had faith that we would get what we hoped for.

Somewhere around that moment we were sure. Our hope was "assured," as verse one says. Then we had faith that we would get to Disneyland. We *knew that we knew*. Something in ourselves concluded that, "Yes. What we have hoped for is certain to occur."

Therefore apparently faith is a place of arrival, rather than something that increases or decreases. It is or it ain't. It's does not grow or diminish like hope does. Chapter 17 in the Book of Luke in the Bible says in verses 5 and 6, the apostles came to Jesus and asked for more faith. But Jesus told them that you don't need *more* faith. There is no *more* or *less* in faith. If you have a bare kernel of faith, even the size of a tiny seed, you could tell a tree to jump in the lake and it would do it! Therefore, Jesus is saying if you have any faith, even merely the size of the tiniest of seeds, then you "have faith;" you have arrived at having faith.

The question becomes how do we get to that place of certainty so that we believe, or "have faith?" First we have to admit that we do nothing perfectly so we will not have faith, or believe, perfectly.

When we flip on a light switch in our homes, we "believe" that the light will go on. Can we categorically prove that it will always go on? No. There always is a chance that what we are sure of will not occur. Thus believing must mean something less than absolute certainty.

When we attempt to sit down in an old, rickety chair, we hope that it will hold us; we are uncertain that it will but we sure hope that it will. However when we sit down in a solid oak chair we are "sure" or "assured" it will hold us. We have faith that it will hold us. Now there may be some unseen crack in the chair which causes us to fall through it when we sit down so our certainty is not an absolute certainty. Yet we still have "faith" in the second chair.

Therefore Jesus did not expect 100% pure faith or certainty for someone to believe that He would heal them. He was aware of the limitations of their imperfect abilities to discern and predict any situation exactly. He must have meant something different from absolute certainty when He said that their "faith" in Him healed them.

During those days, the people talked about His healings and saw them many times, as Jesus passed through their towns which He did more than once. When He came, they could see or hear for themselves that healing miracles were happening often. Whole towns would show up with their sick people and Jesus would heal all of them. Matthew 4:23 says that Jesus went throughout the land teaching and healing every kind of disease and sickness among the people. After seeing and hearing this over and over, individuals" 'hope" for healing shifted to "assuredness" of healing. They grew to have "faith" in His ability to heal them over time.

Did they have 100%, pure faith and certainty that He would heal them? No. They were people who did nothing perfectly. But they were "sure" to the point that they had "faith," which was enough.

Understanding that they did not need perfect faith, how could Jesus heal them? They found the secret in moving from an anxious hoping that Jesus might have mercy on them and perhaps heal them, to a place of peace with a level of certainty in Jesus 'ability and desire to heal them.

Hope has anxiety connected to it. When we hope for something, we are not sure that we will get what we hope for. But faith carries a sense of peace or lack of anxiety. Our hope in the rickety chair successfully holding us up includes anxiety; we are not sure that what we want will happen. But our faith in the solid oak chair holding us eliminates anxiety; we have peace about sitting down in it.

To arrive at this place of peace, we begin with God's love for us. Numerous Scriptures describe God's love for us. The famous passage of John 3:16 says that God loved the world so much that He sent His one and only Son. Chapter four, verse 16, of the Letter of First John says that God is love. To define God is to use one word - love. Therefore if we draw closer to God, we would experience more of His love. As we sit with, hang out with, seek after, walk with, and love God's loving presence more, we naturally feel better about things, about ourselves, and our circumstances. This is hope.

As the darkness of our problems fade, we automatically start seeing some possibilities, and hoping more. We are not sure yet, but we are closer to being sure, that it all just might work out after all. For me, after I slept through the night feeling the loving, comforting arms of Jesus around me, I always awoke with a budding sense of hope.

The famous passage on love in I Corinthians 13 ("Love is patient, love is kind,") ends with the combining of love with hope and faith, that three things remain: faith, hope, love, but the greatest of them is love. Love inextricably connects with hope.

And as hope increases, we become more peaceful. Our anxiety diminishes. Our hope becomes more certain or sure. Eventually, our hope may become faith, the *assurance* of that which you hope for. As we bathe in His love, as we relish it, our hope will grow. This could occur even though our dismal circumstances do not change! We still can enjoy His love, which leads us to trust in that love, and therefore, in Him.

Psalm 46:10 says to be still or peaceful and know that God is God. As we become stilled, or peaceful and not anxious, because of our experiences of the depth of His love, we come to realize just Who we are dealing with here. This is God! God does not dwell within our time and space. God can do anything because God created everything.

Jesus often said that with God, all things are possible; nothing is impossible. As we dwell in His love, we automatically hope in that reality more, which eventually can lead to our trusting in God's ability to fix even our own "impossible" problems.

This teaching helped my hope in God's willingness and ability to solve my impossible problem of cancer to grow and mature. I was headed toward finally believing, having faith in, Jesus being able to heal even me.

CHAPTER 36

Gone!

I decided to give this approach a try. Two or three times every day I would read aloud several healing verses. In my condition, fatigued by a decade-long battle with cancer, still recovering from a bone marrow transplant, recently receiving more of my brother's bone marrow, receiving daily radiation in my leg, and still flooded with various prescription drugs, while simultaneously possessing a heightened sense of spiritual sensitivity, I found these moments enrapturing. I tangibly felt God's Spirit around me.

I could not help but grow in hope. Where love is, hope is. I was on no schedule. It would happen as it would happen. In the meantime I soaked in and enjoyed God's company which really was the ultimate goal anyway.

When good things had happened like the many miracles I experienced already, my hope in God and healing grew. This all moved me toward relaxing and having peace about my cancer, that God could heal me and . . . just maybe . . . would heal me. I was getting to the place of accepting it as true.

I actively had pursued healing by traveling to see and meet those gifted in healing, taking part in healing groups, and learning more about healing. But also I had spent time passively *being* with God, *soaking* in His presence. From all of these experiences I had received a heightened sense of God's love and power, which led to more hope. This momentum moved my sense of hope ever closer to faith in His willingness and ability to heal . . . even me.

As my theology and understanding of God shifted from the comfortable trusting in Jesus who lived in my heart (which was the essence of my faith in God up until my diagnosis) to a more overt, dynamic   heaven-is-with-me-and-will-help-me-in-my-hour-of-need experience, I discovered an explanation for God doing miracles in today's world worked. This new understanding of how faith could change circumstances was proving true for me.

As the days passed I noticed that I could perceptibly feel the cancer's presence in one area of my body around my waist while feeling God's Spirit floating immediately above my right shoulder like one of those circles above someone speaking in a comic book. (This agreed with the words Pastor Christie Pierce who had said over me years earlier that God was three feet away from me.) As I spoke the healing verses aloud I increasingly sensed the cancer in the one place and God's Spirit in the other - always in the same places. This phenomenon continued for weeks.

I persevered in these daily recitations which eventuated into these two forms of *presence* slowly moving closer together. Finally the two discreet phenomenons blended into one! It felt like this nebulous orb of supernatural life was expanding in and around me while simultaneously the cancer was receding. It reminded me of when, as a young boy, I would move forward into the tunnel with my lit matchbooks; the darkness would dissipate and the light would overtake me.

Further, as I found myself in a space of increasing peace I moved toward an increased experience of His Spirit in me doing something miraculous. I never arrived at a place of pure certainty but I did get to an inner sense of an experience of peace and trust (that is, faith) that overcame any anxiety and doubt. Then I palpably felt a power, His power, moving directly against my illness.

In the deep recesses of my spirit I perceived, and even believed, that my cancer was departing my body. I did not understand what was happening nor was consciously certain that my healing had occurred. Yet beyond my reasoning I knew that I knew that healing had come.

Since the Spirit is unseen this incredible phenomenon was unseen. It just happened like a breeze gently blowing into my room.

I did not get too excited as I had not fully comprehended what had happened. Yet I knew. I had a quiet and certain hope. In fact I had faith.

The big miracle that I sought had finally arrived!!

After this experience Dr. Miklos could not find any cancer in my bone marrow, which caused him to get very enthused! The tests showed that my brother's bone marrow and mine were melding successfully and later tests revealed that they had fully merged.

Finally five months after the boost from my brother, Dr. Miklos told me that the lesion was gone as was any sign of cancer in my body. He termed it, "Fantastic!" He even offered to give a testimony about my "amazing" recovery.

It was gone!

The battle was over. My living room prayer experience had become a medical reality.

The blend of my hope becoming faith, the release of God's Spirit from repeating His Word, the prayers of many, the several interactions with those healers, the encouragement of those who loved me, excellent medical care, and the bone marrow transplant with its additional boost had combined to heal me. The original predictions of my living only 11 or 12 years had been disproven 11 years after they were made. My abiding sense that the cancer would not kill me had proven accurate. The accumulation of all these incredible events constituted a major miracle!

Years later when I ran into Dr. Shizuru in the hallway at the Stanford Hospital, we discussed my case. She said that the oncology staff talked about me occasionally since, "We don't know why you survived." She made it clear that the oncologists did not expect the boost from my brother to succeed. It was a desperate, last-ditch attempt to save me. Later she articulated her thoughts as, "Your recovery was pretty remarkable and against the odds in that you did a donor cell infusion [boost] without manipulation [pre-treatment] with your brother's cells already in your body [meaning the boost probably would not *take* because my body was already accustomed to the presence of his cells]. The odds definitely were against you since your cancer had recurred in your **brain** even though your brother's cells were already on board. This comes pretty close to an unexpectedly great outcome. It was better than I could have dreamed of!"

Soon after Dr. Miklos told me the good news I threw out my medicine bottles by the handful. I filled an entire storage box with empty bottles. It struck me how many drugs I had put into my body over the past 11 years. Thousands of pills from hundreds of vials.

Thank God for medication. Thank God for no longer needing to take medication. Thank God for no longer wanting to take medication. Thank God.

I stood there remembering the decade of bad health and noxious drugs; the missed nights out with friends; the skipped adventures of love; the bypassed meaningful conversations; the uncared-for people in need. Missed. A vacant landscape of lost days and nights. Weeds instead of buildings. Space instead of content. Was that my life? I would need time to reflect now that I began to feel well . . .

As I thawed from my convalescence I enjoyed spending time with people more. Life slowly improved. I did not particularly notice that I was different or treated people in a new way. As my years with cancer had been more of a slow-paced endurance walk than a high-pitched battle my recovery was equally subtle. I felt better as time passed. I did not have any euphoric explosions of excitement. My sudden diagnosis was followed by years of quiet adjustment. The somewhat sudden return to good health followed the same path.

But my trust in God had deepened significantly. I learned how much God wanted to exercise awesome power to solve our problems - even the impossible ones!

A year and a half later I finally met her - my wife - at another one of Rita's conferences in Edmonds, Washington. Rita always invited two attendees to stay in her home. Along with me a woman from Australia stayed with her. This woman had sat next to a woman named Sherry on the first day at the conference. That evening while Rita, she, and I were cleaning up the dishes from Rita's dinner the Australian woman raved about this wonderful woman sitting next to her.

Earlier I had told Rita about the small group she had chosen for me. It consisted of people who all seemed to know each other and discussed issues which did not interest me. Rita, in her wisdom, added the two conversations together and moved me into the group which she was leading which happened to include Sherry. She told me that since it only had women in it, it needed a man to "liven things up."

Sherry and I ended up going out to lunch together and while eating hamburgers in my rental car parked next to a golf course I fell in love.

I wrote in my journal how I needed to return to life fully with a whole heart and here she was, the last step in that healing - and the first step into true joy with a wondrous woman.

I ran into Dr. Miklos at a bone marrow transplant survivor reunion at Stanford over nine years after he had told me that the cancer had left my body. He assured me that recurrence of the cancer would never happen, "You won!"

I had staggered through so many days with cancer that I had emotionally become like a bowlegged old cowboy who had ridden through decades of cattle drives. It would take years to let the leathered armor of self-protection slough off my soul to reacquaint myself with myself and others. And it continues.

My shock from the explosion of the "bomb" of my diagnosis led to new territory in my relationship with Jesus, one that included healings and miracles. I was dramatically changed. How do I tell the world what He did for me? One page at a time.

CONCLUSION

One day a friend and I felt particularly brave so we grabbed extra boxes of matchbooks with the intention of pushing further into the unknown darkness of the tunnel beneath my childhood home. We headed off with a more intense sense of purpose and therefore more speed. Because we walked faster we got further before each matchbook burned out.

And then there it was . . . a blush of light.

What seemed like a phantasm of luminescence in the distance brightened at our rapid, excited approach. It was true. We had found light at the end of the tunnel, a break in the tunnel's top where the sun shone in.

As we broke out of the tunnel we found ourselves in someone's backyard only three blocks from where we had started. It had seemed like a much longer distance. We climbed out of the tunnel and crossed through the neighbor's backyard to the street . . . and walked home.

I never went into the tunnel again. The adventure was over. I had made it to the light.

Decades later at one of my college reunions I met a classmate whom I had not known when we were students. It turned out that she was a friend of my older sister, Donna. We enjoyed talking so we later attended a football game together. We had a great time getting thoroughly drenched by a torrential downpour at the game. What better way to watch football?

When we met that day she had surprised me by bringing along one of my dad's old matchbooks. When she had gotten home after meeting me at the reunion, she had found on her kitchen counter one of my father's campaign matchbooks, like I had used to get through the tunnel.

Apparently her daughter who smoked had somehow received the matchbook from Donna who had a penchant for keeping things from the past, including my dad's old matchbooks. For some reason my sister kept some of these matchbooks in her purse even though she did not smoke. She had given one of them to my friend's daughter.

I still have that matchbook in my desk drawer. The matchbook is a tiny reminder of the faithfulness of God to me. It is personal because it has my father's picture on it. It came from a time for me when life was more certain, unhurried, and full of hope. It reminds me of the mythic journeys I took, leaving my street named Mystic and the hoary eucalyptus trees to enter the darkness of the tunnel with only my father's light to show the way.

Also it reminds me I was not alone in the tunnel. I always felt my father's presence in a small way every time I lit a new matchbook. And I felt God's presence in that dark tunnel, as I felt His presence in the darkness of cancer.

POSTSCRIPT

The whole thing surprised me. I did not plan to get cancer, did not plan to seek healing, did not plan to have a bone marrow transplant, and did not plan to find a cure.

As a boy, and even as an adult, my favorite attraction at Disneyland was *Mr. Toad's Wild Ride*. I do not know why. It is not very long or well made. I think I like the craziness. Mr. Toad went on a grand adventure. My cancer had been my own wild ride.

I knew God was faithful yet I did not realize how faithful He could be. And then the miracles. Lots of them. That went beyond faithfulness. They turned the nightmare of cancer into a crazy adventure.

One of my favorite tales about Jesus involves the well-respected religious leader who came to beg Jesus to heal his dying 12-year-old daughter. As Jesus and His entourage were slowly making their way back to the father's home, the father's aides found him with the bad news that she had died. Then Jesus confided in him, "Don't listen to them. Just trust Me." What may have been embarrassing before now was ridiculous. But the father stayed on his wild ride of trusting Jesus to return her to life. And He did! The father went on his crazy adventure and got his miracle. My wild ride to miracles saved my life. What a way to go.

Some friends and I were very fortunate to play varsity high school football for a legitimate tough guy. Our coach, Bob Muenter, would have played for many years as a professional but for a serious injury in a college game. As part of his coaching routine he would meet with the team at someone's home every Thursday night before Friday's game. Those meetings were magic for young, impressionable kids like us.

We sat on the floor or in chairs enraptured by his lessons about life. He dropped simple pearls of wisdom like, "You've got to be yourself." He taught us that authenticity was central to a full life however it turned out. In that pursuit of being our real selves we would find the fulfillment of a well-lived life.

As I immediately learned after my diagnosis I could only live authentically, since I did not have the energy to do anything else. And my true self wanted to live. I could not passively follow medical protocol and merely *hope for the best.*

My dad could not play high school football despite his obvious abilities because his dad could not afford the health insurance costs. So when I played, my dad could not simply sit in the stands and watch the game. He had to get down on the field to be *part of the action.* He brought along a camera to take some pictures (some of which actually turned out okay), to give him an excuse to stand on the sidelines. He had to participate.

That was me. I could not sit in the stands and compliantly watch my cancer play out. I had to turn it into a wild ride on the road to healing, even miraculously.

Now looking through my den window at my rain-soaked garden makes me feel like I am back in the home of my youth. I do not feel nostalgic. I feel familiar. I have lived this moment before.

When I was a boy my family would go to parties hosted by my parents 'friends in wonderful old, large houses that reeked of age, beauty, and stability. The dens were crammed with oak or redwood bookshelves that would transport me to captains 'cabins from 1700s era schooners, creaking and swaying, filled with compasses, sextants, and maps. They felt rich, alive, and full to me, like my den felt to me now.

Sherry is in the next room reading, with our dog lying next to her. She has brought such grace and gratitude into my life. Sacred music is wafting through the house. It is well with my soul. The cancer is gone and forgotten. I dream again. I plan to write more about this healing-spirituality phenomenon.

The promise of Psalm 63:5 that my soul shall be satisfied with marrow and fatness came true. My bone marrow was cured, *fatness* of blessing has returned to my life, and my soul is satisfied.

Years ago I attended a Smothers Brothers concert in a nearby intimate theater, the Fox in Redwood City. The packed house guffawed at every joke and raised eyebrow. Bass playing Dickie still berated older brother, guitar-playing Tommy for his phony stories about his fictitious heroic exploits. They sang their trusty, silly folk songs. And their magic still worked fifty years after their first performances up the road in San Francisco. They ended the evening with a new song, *We're Still Here!* Seemingly nothing had changed.

And now I sit healthy and peaceful. I feel normal again. I'm still here.

So is God.

RESPONSE APPRECIATED

If you feel led, please do me the kindness of writing a review for me at amazon.com. Simply find my book, tap on the box, "Write a customer review," and answer the questions.

If you felt that this book offers hope to people in "impossible" situations, then please pass along the title and subtitle to those in your world, e.g. on your social media and email list. I want to get the word out that there is tangible hope when hope seems to be lost. Thanks.

Also, I would love to hear from you at don@donmulford.com.

FREE GUIDE FOR HELPING SOLVE IMPOSSIBLE PROBLEMS

I have put together a brief guide for copying some of the lessons that I learned about how to solve an impossible problem.

If you would like a free copy of the guide, please send your email address to me using the URL below and I will forward the guide to you.

Simply copy and then paste into the address bar on your computer screen and then provide me with your email address:

https://landing.mailerlite.com/webforms/landing/h3a7j0

I hope that the guide will be of help to you, Don

ABOUT THE AUTHOR

Don Mulford is cured of cancer, which was not supposed to happen. As a minister, chaplain, attorney, and mediator, he has experienced the spiritual and practical. Now he has experienced the miraculous. He lives on the coast in California where he loves to take walks and cycle by the beach, and otherwise hang out with his lovely wife. He plans to write more about the God Who does the impossible and makes it exciting.

Made in the USA
Middletown, DE
30 July 2021

45072729R00106